T 8572

21020

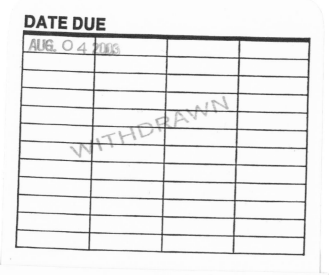

DATE DUE

AUG. 0 4 2003			
		WITHDRAWN	

with

Coping

SOCIAL ANXIETY

Heather Moehn

The Rosen Publishing Group, Inc.
New York

To my husband, Robert Mirman

Published in 2001 by The Rosen Publishing Group, Inc.
29 East 21st Street, New York, NY 10010

First Edition

Cover photo by Ira Fox

Library of Congress Cataloging-in-Publication Data

Moehn, Heather.
Coping with social anxiety / by Heather Moehn.
p. cm. — (Coping)
Includes bibliographical references and index.
ISBN 0-8239-3363-6
1. Social phobia—Juvenile literature. 2. Anxiety—Juvenile literature.
[1. Social phobia. 2. Anxiety.] I. Title. II. Series.
RC552.S62 M64 2001
616.85'223—dc21

210 20   2001000589

Manufactured in the United States of America

Contents

Introduction

Kathy's teachers view her as a good student who always does her homework but rarely participates in class. Her close friends see her as a loyal and trustworthy person who is a lot of fun once you get to know her. The other students in school think she is shy and very quiet.

None of them realize how much Kathy struggles with everyday life. When teachers call on her in class, her heart races, her face gets red and hot, and she forgets what she wants to say.

Kathy believes that people think she is stupid and inadequate. She imagines that classmates and teachers talk behind her back about the silly things she says. She makes excuses not to go to social events because she is terrified she will do something awkward. Staying home while her friends are out having a good time also upsets her. "Why can't I just act like other people?" she often thinks.

Although Kathy feels isolated, she has a very common problem—social anxiety. Literally millions of people are so affected by self-consciousness that they have difficulties in social situations. For some, the anxiety occurs during very specific events, such as giving a speech or eating in public. For others, like Kathy, social anxiety is part of everyday life.

Unfortunately, social anxiety is not an easily diagnosed condition. Instead, it is often viewed as the far edge of a continuum of behaviors and feelings that occur during social situations. Although you may not have as much difficulty as Kathy, shyness may still be causing you distress, affecting your relationships, or making you act in ways with which you are not happy. If this is the case, you will benefit from the advice and techniques provided in this book.

The good news is that it is possible to change your thinking and behavior. However, there are no easy solutions. It takes strong motivation and time to overcome social anxiety. It might even be necessary to see a professional therapist or take medication. Eventually, becoming free of your anxiety will make the hard work well worth the effort.

This book will help you understand social anxiety and the impact it can have on your life, now and in the future. You will find out how the disorder is diagnosed, you will receive information on professional guidance, and you will learn ways to cope with and manage the symptoms. Becoming an extroverted person is probably unlikely, but you can become more confident in social situations and increase your self-esteem.

Social Anxiety

Shyness is not necessarily a problem. It can be a very nice aspect of your personality. Many introverted celebrities, such as Chelsea Clinton and the late Princess Diana, are considered sophisticated and classy because of their reserved personalities.

Shyness can make you appear intelligent, discreet, and circumspect. Shy people are valued as good listeners and are more likely to be considered kindhearted, conscientious, and trustworthy. They rarely are overaggressive or obnoxious and usually try not to act in ways that hurt others. A degree of shyness also allows you to be cautious and judge situations before jumping into them. You can stand back, observe, make careful decisions, and then act deliberately.

With all of these positive qualities, it is no surprise that between 10 and 20 percent of those who consider themselves shy like their personalities and don't want to change. They are comfortable with being quiet and are confident that when they do have something to say others will pay attention.

Distinguishing social anxiety from normal shyness is sometimes difficult. It has to do with the level of distress and impairment associated with social fears. If you prefer being quiet and listening to others and you feel comfortable with that role, you probably don't have social anxiety. On the other hand, if you don't speak up because you are afraid others won't like what you say or you are terrified of sounding foolish, you most likely have a degree of social anxiety.

The History of Social Anxiety

The fact that some people are shyer than others has been observed since ancient times. However, the medical community didn't become interested in this condition until the 1970s, when Philip Zimbardo founded the Stanford Shyness Clinic.

At the time, many professionals believed that shyness was a natural state that children eventually outgrew. Zimbardo showed that shyness actually is a widespread psychological problem that has deep and lasting effects on those who suffer from it.

This new awareness led to a great deal of research into the causes and treatment of social anxiety. Today, the condition is in the spotlight. Ads in magazines and commercials on television tell about social anxiety and advertise medications to treat it. People are becoming more open about discussing when they feel anxious and feel less ashamed about asking for help. The time has never been better for you to try to overcome your social anxiety.

Who Suffers?

If you have social anxiety, you are not alone. The National Comorbidity Study found social phobia to be the third most common psychiatric disorder, after major depression and alcohol dependence. Experts believe that millions of people suffer from it. It is difficult to get exact numbers because the nature of social anxiety often makes it difficult for people to seek help. Many people who appear confident and strong suffer silently for years before telling anyone how they feel.

In the general population, social anxiety appears to affect more women than men. This may be due in part to the social norms that determine that women should be less aggressive and more reserved than men. However, more men seek treatment, possibly because social anxiety has more of an impact on the jobs traditionally held by men. As gender roles in society continue to shift, these statistics will probably change.

When Does Social Anxiety Appear?

Social anxiety can develop at any age. Many people remember feeling afraid during social situations as early as kindergarten. Others don't develop symptoms until they are adults. However, social anxiety most commonly appears in adolescence, between the ages of 15 and 20. When you think about the changes that are taking place in your life at this time, this fact makes a lot of sense.

As a teenager, you are expected to act more like an adult than a child. You are beginning to take on adult responsibilities and see yourself as a part of society. Meeting the expectations of others and making a good impression are very important. As a result, you may worry about what others think of you and be afraid of acting incorrectly.

Types of Social Anxiety

Just as people's personalities are unique, no two cases of social anxiety are alike. Your distress undoubtedly has different triggers, symptoms, and reasons than anyone else's. Take a few moments to think about the situations in which you feel the most anxious. You may find that there are only a few specific activities that cause stress, and that you are comfortable at most other times. You might realize that you feel anxious in almost every interaction you encounter. Experts have determined that there are two main categories into which most cases of social anxiety fall: specific social anxiety and generalized social anxiety.

Specific Social Anxiety

Specific social anxiety is when you experience stress about a certain task or event. There are many situations in which fears may appear, but the most common involve performance anxiety: the belief that you will perform a task or behavior in an incorrect or unacceptable manner. Let's examine a few forms of specific social anxiety in more detail.

Fear of Public Speaking

Public speaking is often ranked as the most commonly feared experience in the United States. Some people are able to work through their fears and often say the nervousness helps them perform better. For others, speaking in public is a terrifying experience that is to be avoided at all times. This specific social anxiety almost prevented Joel from graduating with his class.

A class in public speaking is required at my high school. Most kids take it when they are freshmen, just to get it out of the way. I signed up for it every semester, but just thinking about giving a speech made me nervous. I imagined that I would forget my lines or say something wrong. I was in agony until I dropped the class.

Finally, during my senior year, the speech teacher called me into his office. He described the symptoms of anxiety and asked if that was why I always dropped the class. I couldn't believe that he knew how I felt and that so many other people have the same problem. He offered to meet with me privately to help me rehearse and overcome my anxiety. I definitely wasn't the best speaker, but I managed to pass the class.

If you are afraid of public speaking, Joel's worries are probably similar to your own. You also might be afraid people will be bored or not like what you are saying. You probably are concerned that people will notice how anxious you are and will see your hands trembling or will hear your voice quiver. You might worry that you will sound foolish or will not be able to answer someone's question.

Public speaking is hard to avoid. Whether it is giving a presentation, leading a class discussion, or participating in a meeting, being able to talk to a group of people is an important life skill.

Fear of Taking Tests

Maree is a smart student and always does well on written assignments and research papers. But because of her fear of taking tests, she usually ends up with Cs. She feels all of her hard work is for nothing and is extremely discouraged with school. She studies diligently for every exam and usually knows the material inside and out. As soon as she enters the classroom, though, her mind goes blank. When she gets the test, she is so nervous that she can barely write her name. Lately, on test days, she pretends to be sick.

Many people feel intense anxiety about tests. A similar problem is known as writer's block. Journalists and professional writers aren't the only people who experience writer's block. You may deal with it when you have to answer essay questions on a test, write a paper, or compose a cover letter for a job application.

The fear in test anxiety and writer's block is that what you produce will be inadequate and unacceptable. You are so worried about what others will think of your abilities that you are unable to concentrate on the task. Often, the more important the test or written work, the greater the anxiety you feel.

Fear of Shopping

Because teens are one of the largest consumer groups in America, it is often assumed that they all love to shop. For many people, however, a trip to the mall is an agonizing event.

People with anxiety about shopping are afraid of being judged based on what they select. They feel so self-conscious that they don't even see what they are looking at as they browse. They have the sensation that they are going to be confronted at any time.

The thought of making small talk with a store clerk is terrifying. In order not to appear unreasonable or uncooperative, they often make purchases they don't want, then agonize about returning the items.

Some people avoid this fear by ordering what they want on the Internet or from catalogs. Although online shopping may make purchasing items easier, it is not always feasible. What if your parents ask you to run to the store for milk or toilet paper? What if you need special supplies for a project at school the next day?

Once you live on your own and become responsible for providing your basic necessities, it becomes even more difficult to survive with this specific anxiety. A strong fear of shopping could limit your independence.

Fear of Talking on the Telephone

Along with shopping, talking on the phone is something people assume teens love to do. However, people suffering from this specific social anxiety constantly avoid the telephone. Tamar explains her fear:

> I never answer the phone myself. Whenever some-one calls me, whoever answers the phone has to find out who is calling and why. Then, I'm able to prepare myself a little bit. I'm always afraid that I am going to say the wrong thing. Those pauses in conversation drive me crazy. I always imagine that the other person is thinking about how ridiculous I sound.

The degree of anxiety people feel often relates to the type of conversation. Routine calls, such as asking what time a movie starts or ordering a pizza, usually are handled with little stress. Conversations that could move in unanticipated directions are much more difficult. Examples of this type of call include chatting with an acquaintance or answering the phone when you don't know who the caller is. The hardest calls tend to be those that involve evaluation, such as speaking with a boss, teacher, or potential date.

Like many of the other specific social anxieties, it is difficult to avoid talking on the telephone. Although answering machines and voice mail may seem like good options, your friends and family will get frustrated if they never speak to you directly. In the work force, not answering your phone can have a negative impact on your performance, which affects salary increases and promotions.

Fear of Eating in Public

Eating anyplace where others might be watching is another situation in which social anxiety often occurs. If you have this specific social anxiety, you might be afraid that people will notice your hands tremble as you hold your fork. You also might worry that you are going to spill food on yourself, or worse, on others. For William, this fear developed after a bad experience.

A friend of my father's hired me to do odd jobs around his law office last summer. On my first day, he took me out to lunch at a deli across the street. While we were eating, I knocked over my soda. It spilled all over our sandwiches and ran off the table onto Mr. Taylor's expensive suit. I was so embarrassed. If he didn't know my dad, I probably would have run out of the restaurant and would never have returned to work again. Now, whenever I go out to eat with someone, I only order food, even when I am really thirsty. If I do end up with a drink, I blush and get really nervous. I am so sure that I am going to spill it that my hands shake when I try to pick it up.

14

If you experience anxiety while eating in public, your social life is probably suffering. In our culture, food is associated with just about every major holiday and celebration. Think about Thanksgiving with its elaborate dinner, birthdays with cake and ice cream, and parties with snacks and drinks. Eating and drinking are unavoidable.

Fear of Using Public Rest Rooms

Fear of using public rest rooms is another common social anxiety. Many people who have "bashful bladders" are too embarrassed to tell anyone, which can make the problem worse. As with the other specific anxieties, this one causes people to focus on what others think and the judgments they may make.

For women, using a rest room when there is a line can be very difficult. You might be afraid of taking too long, or making other people in the line angry. You may be embarrassed by the sounds you make that are perfectly normal.

In men's rest rooms, using a urinal can cause a great deal of anxiety. Troy has this problem in school. Because all the students use the rest rooms between classes, he is rarely there alone. As he stands at a urinal, he worries. "What if people think I'm a pervert? Are they wondering what I am doing?" These thoughts make him more self-conscious, which makes it even more difficult for him to urinate.

Many people with this anxiety limit their social lives so they won't be too far from home and their own bathrooms. At school or work, they may search for out-of-the-way rest rooms that are rarely used or try to take their breaks at times when fewer people are likely to be in the rest rooms. It is common for people with this social anxiety to avoid drinking fluids during the day to limit the number of times they need to use the rest room, which is not healthy.

Generalized Social Anxiety

In contrast to people with specific social anxieties, you may be afraid in a wide variety of situations. You might feel that people are judging everything you do and you might set unreasonable standards of perfection for yourself. This condition is called generalized (or discrete) social anxiety. Generalized social anxiety accounts for 80 percent of all cases of social anxiety.

Often, people with generalized social anxiety get caught in a vicious cycle. Because they are overly anxious in many situations, they act in clumsy and awkward ways, which in turn makes them feel even more discouraged and anxious. This cycle often results in depression and chronic stress.

Generalized social anxiety can affect almost every aspect of your life. This has been the case for Toni, a college senior.

In high school, I hardly had any friends. I didn't participate in any extracurricular activities and managed to get by with average grades. Because I attend a large state university, I am even more invisible. So far, I have avoided any class that has any interaction with my peers, such as discussion groups or labs.

As graduation approaches, I need to decide what type of career I want. The thought of job interviews

Are you publicly or privately shy?

If you are publicly shy, you will agree with the following types of statements that focus on how others view you.

- ➥ I'm concerned about my style of doing things.

- ➥ I worry about my appearance.

- ➥ I want to make a good impression.

If you are privately shy, you will agree with the following types of statements that focus on how you view yourself.

- ➥ I'm always trying to figure myself out.

- ➥ I constantly scrutinize my feelings and motives.

- ➥ I notice changes in my mood easily.

terrifies me. I am considering grad school but would need recommendations to apply. I haven't even spoken to most of my professors, and the ones who know me probably can't say anything good about me.

As a result, I'm really depressed. When I imagine the future, I can't see myself being happy. I'll probably move back to my parents' house after graduation. I know they are disappointed in me, and that makes me feel like a complete failure.

Self-Consciousness

In addition to the divisions of specific and generalized social anxiety, experts also identify two types of self-consciousness: public self-consciousness and private self-consciousness. Although self-awareness and self-insight are positive traits in healthy personalities, in people with social anxiety this awareness becomes extreme and obsessive.

Publicly self-conscious people are extremely aware of what others think of them. They worry about how they appear and the impression they are making. Many publicly shy people describe feeling distanced from an event in which they are participating. For instance, while they are speaking with someone, they are constantly evaluating and editing how they act and what they say. As a result, they feel they do not fully take part in any activities.

Imagine you are going to a party with a popular group of people. If you are publicly shy, you would worry all afternoon about what you were going to wear and what others will think of you. When you finally walk into the party, you notice that two of the people you admire are wearing khakis and button-down shirts, and you immediately feel out of place in your jeans and T-shirt. You think everyone is watching you and wondering why you are there when it is obvious you don't belong. When someone attempts to speak with you, you are so overwhelmed that you can stutter only a brief reply before running to the rest room.

By contrast, if you are a privately shy person, you can appear at ease in social situations. At the same party, you might be able to tell jokes and be the center of attention, while internally you are in turmoil.

Privately self-conscious people are more concerned about protecting how they feel than about how others view them. Sometimes, they try to hide their fears by being loud and talkative. Many comedians, actors, and singers are privately shy people. They are able to mask their feelings of inadequacy, but they feel phony and lack true self-confidence.

No matter whether you have specific or generalized social anxiety or are publically or privately shy, social anxiety has a strong impact on your life. In the next chapters, you learn how to determine if you have social anxiety and how you are affected by it.

Do You Have
Social Anxiety?

Any degree of social anxiety affects the way you think, the way you feel, and the way you act. This chapter describes how your mind and body respond to social anxiety and how this condition influences your behavior. It also describes how a diagnosis is made and explains why it is often difficult to determine if you have social anxiety.

Social Anxiety and Your Mind

Your most powerful thoughts are often unconscious and are based upon deeply held beliefs. In social anxiety, these thoughts are usually negative and ineffective. Examples of ways in which your mind is affected by social anxiety include faulty core beliefs, inaccurate expectations, negative automatic thoughts, and perfectionism. Let's look more closely at each of these examples.

Core Beliefs

All of us have core beliefs that influence our behavior and how we feel about ourselves. Often you think of them as an "unwritten law." You may have developed your beliefs through experience, or they may have come from your parents, your religion, or your culture.

Although you may not realize it, your core beliefs are always in your mind and affect everything you do. They are the guidelines according to which you judge everything in your life. When your core beliefs are positive, you are confident and believe you can accomplish great things. Examples of positive core beliefs include:

➯ I am intelligent.

➯ My mistakes are a learning experience.

➯ I believe in myself.

When the core beliefs are negative, however, they prevent you from getting what you want from life. Examples of negative core beliefs common in social anxiety include:

➯ I am never going to be successful.

➯ Everyone must like me.

➯ If I am not liked, I am worthless.

➯ I can't trust anyone.

Because negative core beliefs have been such a deep part of your personality, it may take a lot of work to become aware of what they are. As you become more conscious of them, you probably will realize that they are unrealistic, and that you are basing your anxiety on false beliefs.

Yvonne's parents died in a car accident when she was a baby. She was raised by her grandmother, who firmly believed that children should be seen and not heard. Whenever Yvonne ran around the house or played loudly, her grandmother would yell at her to "act like a lady." Because her grandmother didn't want many children in her house, she never encouraged Yvonne to make friends.

When Yvonne started school, she was very timid. She was afraid of the other children, who seemed loud and aggressive. Now in high school, Yvonne doesn't have many friends. She is extremely bashful and is too afraid to speak with her classmates. Because of the way she was raised, her main core belief is that good behavior means being quiet. Because her classmates often ignore her, another core belief is that people aren't interested in her thoughts and opinions. These two beliefs make it difficult for Yvonne to overcome her social anxiety.

Inaccurate Expectations

When you have negative, unrealistic beliefs, you probably have inaccurate expectations of what will occur in a situation. This type of thinking is often called "catastrophizing."

People with social anxiety generally have two areas in which they "catastrophize." The first is when they feel that the threat posed by an event is much greater than it is in reality. In other words, they overestimate the danger of social situations. For instance, when Mariah takes the first biology test of the year, she feels that her whole education is riding on that one exam. She believes that the teacher is judging her intelligence. She believes the teacher will think of her as either stupid or smart for the rest of the semester, based upon her performance on this one test. She puts a tremendous amount of pressure on herself for reasons of which others are completely unaware. As a result, she fears taking tests.

The second inaccurate expectation is that the consequences of their actions are far more severe than they are in reality. For example, when Mariah gets a *D* on the biology exam because her fear of taking tests made her freeze, she believes she is going to flunk biology, not get accepted into medical school, and never realize her dream of becoming a pediatrician. To other people, one test is seen as a small part of the overall grade, but because of her social anxiety, Mariah believes that the consequences will haunt her forever.

Automatic Thoughts

All people have ongoing thoughts running through their heads. You probably have these thoughts so often that they feel "automatic" and beyond your control. Many times, these thoughts are positive and pleasant. For instance, when you are wearing an outfit you know looks good on you, you have unconscious thoughts about feeling happy with your appearance. Other examples of positive automatic thoughts include:

⇝ People want to hear my opinion.

⇝ What I have to say is important.

⇝ I am good at what I do.

At other times, such as in social situations where you are experiencing anxiety, these thoughts are negative and are accompanied by strong emotions. If you start keeping track of these thoughts, you may be surprised at what they are. Some examples of thoughts typical of people with social anxiety include:

- ☞ I don't fit in.

- ☞ I sound stupid.

- ☞ Nobody wants to listen to me.

- ☞ I look out of place.

- ☞ I'm ruining it.

- ☞ I'm such a loser.

Psychologists call this type of thinking irrational and maladaptive. It is irrational because it is not based on reality, and it is maladaptive because it does not help you cope. In fact, irrational thoughts often make the anxiety worse.

When Roosevelt's class went on a field trip, he was thrilled to be sitting next to a group of popular athletes on the bus. He had always admired the group and had longed to become friends with them. Unfortunately, Roosevelt suffers from social anxiety and doesn't have strong self-esteem. During the entire bus ride, he automatically thought, "I don't fit in. They'll never accept me." These negative thoughts made him feel awkward and uncomfortable. He was unable to speak with anyone and spent most of the ride staring out the window.

Once, when the group began talking about what football team was going to be in the Super Bowl,

Roosevelt started to make a comment about his favorite team, the Minnesota Vikings. When he realized everyone near him was listening to what he was saying, he became very self-conscious. He began to think, "I'm blowing it. I sound like an idiot." These thoughts made him feel even worse. He quickly stumbled through what he wanted to say and went back to looking out the window. "I'm such a loser," he told himself.

In addition to the fear that occurs when you are in a stressful situation, simply anticipating the event may be a major problem as well. Many people with social anxiety have negative automatic thoughts about an event for weeks or even months before it occurs. For instance, if you have a few lines in the school play that will be performed in three months, you might tell yourself during all of this time that you will never be good enough and that you are probably going to sound stupid. Such thoughts are self-defeating. Their negativity might make you spend less time preparing and might make you feel extremely nervous, problems that definitely will affect your performance.

Maladaptive Thinking Patterns

Maladaptive thinking patterns are quite common in all types of people, no matter what their situation. Often, people don't even realize the impact their mindset has on the way they perceive a situation. A list of the most common types of maladaptive thinking problems, with examples of how the mindsets can contribute to social anxiety, follows this section. Do you recognize some of your thinking patterns?

All-or-nothing thinking is when you see things as only black or white and either-or. For example, if you make a mistake while giving a speech, you think you are a total failure; or if a friend acts distant on the telephone, you believe he or she doesn't like you anymore.

Labeling is an extension of all-or-nothing thinking. When you make a mistake, instead of accepting that you made an error, you label yourself an idiot. If your girlfriend or boyfriend breaks up with you, instead of realizing that he or she doesn't love you, you call yourself unlovable.

Overgeneralizing is basing conclusions on isolated events, then applying them across diverse situations. If you spill a soda, you think, "I'm always a klutz." If you can't think of something to say when introduced to someone new, you think, "I never make a good impression." The tip-off to this type of thinking is use of the words "always" or "never."

Mental filtering is when you remember and dwell on only the negative elements of an event. For instance, after a party, you remember the awkward pauses in conversations, feeling uncomfortable, and forgetting people's names, while you forget all moments when you had good conversations, introduced yourself to someone new, and when someone paid you a compliment.

Discounting the positive is somewhat related to mental filtering. It is when you do something well, such as give a good speech, but make excuses like "It doesn't count" or "Anyone could have done it" and feel the accomplishment wasn't good enough.

Jumping to conclusions is making negative interpretations about events when there is no evidence to support them. There are generally two forms of jumping to conclusions. In "mind reading," you believe that someone is reacting negatively to you without checking it out. For instance, if two people stop their conversation when you walk up to them, you assume that they were gossiping about you. In "fortune telling," you anticipate that things will turn out badly. If you fear taking tests, for example, you always feel that you will fail, even before you start the test.

Magnification is exaggerating the importance of problems. For instance, if you don't do well on a test, you believe you are going to fail the entire semester.

Emotional reasoning is when you mistake your emotions for reality. For example, you feel lonely; therefore, you think no one likes you.

"Should" and "shouldn't" statements are ways of thinking that make you feel that you are never good enough. Even though you do well on a job interview, you think, "I should have said this," or "I shouldn't have said that." Other words that indicate this type of thinking are "ought to" and "have to."

Personalizing the blame is holding yourself responsible for things beyond your control. For instance, you are on your way to study with a group of classmates and you get stuck in traffic. Instead of realizing and accepting that the traffic problem is out of your control, you think you are irresponsible because you are going to be late.

Perfectionism

People with social anxiety tend to be perfectionists. A degree of perfectionism is generally seen as a good trait. It makes people strive to do the best they can. Perfectionists have an eye for mistakes that often escape the notice of other people. They are very successful students and do well in the workplace.

However, perfectionism can be taken too far. If you are a perfectionist, you probably set unrealistic goals for yourself. When you are unable to meet your expectations, you feel let down and depressed. You may feel that no matter how hard you try, you will never be good enough.

Social anxiety becomes worse when you are a perfectionist. Expecting to act perfectly in every situation puts great pressure on you. If you feel you need to make a great impression every time you meet someone, if you want to say something brilliant every time you open your mouth, or if you want everyone to love you, you are setting yourself up for great disappointments.

The pressures associated with perfectionism and social anxiety can keep you from succeeding and being happy. They result in the fear of making mistakes, stress from the pressure to perform, and extreme self-consciousness. Perfectionism also causes tension, frustration, disappointment, anger, and sadness.

Social Anxiety and Your Body

The physical symptoms of social anxiety are very uncomfortable. When you are anxious, your body thinks you are in danger and tries to tell you to take action. The physical responses range from an uneasy and uncomfortable sensation to a full-blown anxiety attack. When you experience any form of anxiety, it is common to feel like everyone can see your nervousness and the way it is affecting you. In reality, the symptoms are not as obvious to other people. Some common physical responses to social anxiety include:

- Shortness of breath

- Rapid heart rate

- Trembling or shaking

- Sweating

- Blushing

- "Butterflies" in your stomach

- Dizziness

- "Ringing" in your ears

Depending on the situation, you may feel one or all of these symptoms in various intensities. You may also have other reactions that you could add to this list.

Besides the physical responses to an anxiety-causing situation, you may feel chronic stress or tension. Many people with social anxiety go through life in a constant state of anxiety. When you are always on your guard around others and are worrying about things that are out of your control, your body experiences a great deal of stress. Being tense most of the time often results in stomachaches, headaches, chronic fatigue, muscle stiffness, and other stress-related symptoms.

Your Behavioral Responses to Anxiety

The ways in which people react to social situations are often a result of physical and mental responses. Feeling anxious is a clue from your body that you are in danger and need to take action. However, because the danger is exaggerated, your actions often do not fit the situation and do not help you. Two typical behaviors are freezing and avoidance.

When people freeze in a situation, they cannot react. Movement, speech, and memory are all affected. You may have experienced freezing when a teacher called on you in class. When attention like that was placed upon you, you probably felt the physical responses of blushing, shortness of breath, and rapid heart rate, among others. You probably had negative thoughts running through your head, such as "I'm such an idiot. I look stupid." As a result of the strong physical and mental reactions, you froze and were unable to remember the answer; perhaps you could not speak at all.

Because feelings of anxiety are unpleasant, some people try to avoid stressful situations altogether. If you are nervous around crowds of people, you may avoid going to parties or dances. If you are afraid of speaking in public, you probably avoid classes or situations in which you would be asked to speak or make a presentation.

There are also other, subtler forms of avoidance. If you are nervous in crowds, you may not avoid parties entirely, but you might leave early or latch onto one person the entire time. Or, you may distract yourself by daydreaming or flipping through CDs instead of talking with people.

> *Because of her social anxiety, Ruby hadn't partici-*
> *pated in any extracurricular activities during high*
> *school. At the beginning of her senior year, her guid-*
> *ance counselor told her she would have a better*
> *chance of getting into her top-choice college if she*
> *would join activities, so she joined the Spanish club.*
>
> *The group was led by the Spanish teacher and*
> *met once a week before school. When Ruby joined,*
> *they were beginning to plan the annual fiesta, and*
> *there were many decisions to make. At first, the*
> *other students tried to include her and would ask*
> *her opinion about decorations or games, but Ruby*
> *was so anxious that she couldn't respond. Soon,*
> *they stopped asking and left her alone.*
>
> *Ruby thought she was being a part of the group*
> *simply by showing up, but she never volunteered for*
> *any of the planning committees and never offered*
> *suggestions. When it was time to fill out college*
> *applications, Ruby asked the Spanish teacher to write*
> *her a recommendation. The teacher said she couldn't*
> *because she didn't know Ruby well enough.*

Patterns of avoidance may be so deeply ingrained in your lifestyle that you are not even aware that you are exhibiting them. Think carefully about your reactions to various situations. When you receive an invitation, do you instantly think of reasons why you can't accept? When you are with a group of people, do you use escape mechanisms, such as reading a magazine, hiding in the restroom, or daydreaming?

Avoidance may help lessen your anxiety in the moment, but in the long run, it usually makes things worse. Life is very unsatisfying when you avoid so many situations, and such behavior hurts self-esteem and self-confidence.

How Is Social Anxiety Diagnosed?

Unfortunately, there is no test to determine whether you have social anxiety. Diagnosis is often complicated by the reluctance of socially anxious patients to discuss personal information with doctors. It is very important that you are completely honest with your doctor, and that he or she listens carefully to how you describe your feelings. In many ways, the doctor is like a detective finding clues about your inner world and then putting those clues together to figure out the problem. Once he or she decides that social anxiety may be the issue, he or she can refer to case histories, new research information, and insights from other professionals.

Misdiagnosis

Because there are so many types of anxiety disorders, it is sometimes difficult for therapists to make an accurate diagnosis. Often, social anxiety is masked by other anxiety disorders, such as panic disorder or generalized anxiety disorder. It is also sometimes misdiagnosed as a depressive disorder or personality disorder.

Problems with diagnosis can also occur if your doctor was trained before social anxiety became a category in the *Diagnostic Statistical Manual of Mental Disorders* (DSM) in 1979. (The *DSM* is the official diagnostic manual of the American Psychiatric Association. It lists all the known psychiatric conditions and their symptoms.) For these professionals, social anxiety is not a familiar diagnosis. It was only after 1979 that it was recognized as a treatable condition. This reason for misdiagnosis is becoming less common as social anxiety receives more publicity and is becoming more well recognized.

The Brief Social Phobia Scale

Jonathon Davidson, the director of the Anxiety and Traumatic Stress Program at Duke University, developed the Brief Social Phobia Scale (BSPS) to help determine whether someone suffers from social anxiety. The BSPS has two parts: fear/avoidance and physiology. When you take it, think about how you reacted to each situation during the past week. If you haven't been in a particular situation, imagine how you would react. This is especially important if you haven't experienced a situation because you are avoiding it.

In the fear and avoidance section, rate how much fear certain situations cause and how common your avoidance of the situations is. The physiologic section rates the physical symptoms you may experience in social anxiety, such as blushing, trembling, or sweating. If you never experience the particular symptom, give it zero. If you experience it in an extreme amount, rate it a four.

When you have completed the survey, add up all the rankings. A higher score means that you probably suffer from social anxiety. The BSPS can be used as a self-rating, but it is most effective when used as a starting point when you talk to your doctor.

Brief Social Phobia Scale (BSPS)

Part I (Fear/Avoidance)

How much do you fear and avoid the following situations?

	FEAR	AVOIDANCE
1. Speaking in public or in front of others.	☐	☐
2. Talking to people in authority.	☐	☐
3. Talking to strangers.	☐	☐
4. Being embarrassed or humiliated.	☐	☐
5. Being criticized.	☐	☐
6. Attending social gatherings.	☐	☐
7. Doing something while being watched (this does not include speaking).	☐	☐

Clinical Anchor Points
Fear:
0 = None
1 = Mild = Infrequent and/or not distressing
2 = Moderate = Frequent and/or some distress
3 = Severe = Constant, dominating a person's life and/or clearly distressing
4 = Extreme = Incapacitating and/or very painfully distressing

Avoidance
0 = Never (0%)
1 = Rare (1–33%)
2 = Sometimes (34–66%)
3 = Frequent (67–99%)
4 = Always (100%)

Part II (Physiology)

When you are in a situation that involves contact with other people, or when you are thinking about such a situation, do you experience the following symptoms?
Record in each box below a score corresponding with the following anchor points.

PHYSIOLOGICAL

1. Blushing ☐

2. Palpitations ☐

3. Trembling or shaking ☐

4. Sweating ☐

Clinical Anchor Points
Physiological:
0 = None
1 = Mild = Infrequent and/or not distressing
2 = Moderate = Frequent and/or some distress
3 = Severe = Constant, dominating a person's life and/or clearly distressing
4 = Extreme = Incapacitating and/or very painfully distressing

Total Scores

Part I   Fear Items (1–7)   Total_____(F)
          Avoidance Items (1–7)   Total_____(A)

Part II   Physiological Items (1–4) Total_____(P)

          (F + A + P)   TOTAL _____

What Causes Social Anxiety?

If you recognized your behavior in the descriptions of social anxiety, you may be asking "Why me?" or "How did I get this way?" These are not easy questions to answer. After decades of research about anxiety, experts still do not know exactly what causes some people to develop social anxiety. They suspect that a combination of biochemical, genetic, and environmental factors may be involved.

Origins of Anxiety

Imagine that you are walking down an unfamiliar street in a bad part of town late at night. Suddenly, you hear footsteps behind you. How would your body react? Typically, you would tense up and your heart would race. You might feel cold but be perspiring at the same time. All of your senses would be focused on the footsteps and the danger they may present.

In this type of situation, feeling anxious is perfectly normal. When you sense danger, your body instinctively prepares to protect you, whether by facing the danger head-on or by running away from it as fast as you can. This reaction is called the fight-or-flight response and goes back to the beginning of human evolution. Today, even though we don't face as many life-threatening situations, the fight-or-flight instinct remains part of our bodies' nervous systems.

As a result, you may feel the physical symptoms, such as shortness of breath and rapid heart rate, during moments that are not a real threat. In social anxiety, these symptoms typically occur during situations in which you fear people's judgments and worry that you will behave in ways that are embarrassing. Although events such as walking into a party alone or answering a question in class can be stressful at times, they are relatively safe situations that shouldn't cause the fight-or-flight response.

Biochemistry

Your brain is the center of communication in your body. It sends messages that tell you when you are tired, excited, hungry, or happy. To keep everything running smoothly, billions of brain cells constantly talk to each other through a complex network of interconnecting cells. The cells don't actually touch each other. Instead, information is passed between them by way of chemical messengers called neurotransmitters.

Neurotransmitters

There are many different kinds of neurotransmitters which are used for different types of messages. For instance, when you cut your finger with a sharp knife, you usually don't feel the pain immediately. Then, your finger starts to tingle and you feel lightheaded. This reaction occurs because your brain recognizes a crisis and sends out beta-endorphin, the neurotransmitter that eases pain. When you are alone on a dark and deserted street and hear footsteps, the neurotransmitter for fear is sent from your brain and your body responds appropriately, either by fighting or by running away.

When you have social anxiety, however, the neurotransmitters associated with fear do not flow properly. Too many chemicals may be released or they may be released at inappropriate times. Or a reasonable amount of chemicals may be released at an appropriate time, but you may be overly sensitive to them. As a result of these abnormalities, the neurotransmitters set off false alarms and make you feel that you are in danger when, in reality, you are not.

A fact that seems to support the biochemistry theory is that social anxiety does not go away over time. In fact, for many people, the symptoms worsen with age. Adults who have been socially anxious since childhood often feel ashamed about the condition because they believe they should "grow out of it." However, if there is a biochemical reason for the condition, medication may be needed to regulate the system. This is why it is important to talk to your doctor about social anxiety.

Genetics

Genes are often referred to as the blueprint for human beings. It is well-known that they determine such things as eye color, hair texture, the shape of your nose, and other traits inherited from your parents. Actually, genes are responsible for much more than physical characteristics.

You may be someone who cries easily, can't stand loud noises, and hates crowds, while other people you know don't seem to cry in any situation, love loud events, and thrive in a crowd. This may result from genetics. Although a specific gene for shyness and social anxiety does not exist, many experts feel that there are genes that control how emotional and sensitive people are. In general, it seems that people with social anxiety are more emotional and highly sensitive to things such as loud noises and chaotic crowds.

Because you can't change your genetic makeup, you probably won't transform into the most outgoing person in your class or suddenly love to be the center of attention. However, you can learn how to manage your shyness and feel more comfortable. The situation is similar to a characteristic such as body type. If your parents are short with large frames and you are short with a large frame, you might be able to change some aspects of the way you look through diet and exercise, but you will never become tall and waiflike.

Evidence that supports the genetic theory is that anxiety often runs in families, just like blue eyes or curly hair. Children who have social anxiety often realize that their parents also have a difficult time in social situations. A genetic influence is tricky to prove, however, because many aspects of social anxiety may be learned behaviors.

Environment

The biochemical and genetic explanations for social anxiety are fairly straightforward. However, they don't explain why one person fears all social situations while another fears speaking in public and yet another is afraid only of talking on the phone. The environment is generally considered the final factor that determines social anxiety. In other words, when a person has a biochemical and genetic predisposition to anxiety, the form that anxiety takes may depend on the circumstances of his or her life.

Your environment includes where you live, the people you live with, your school, and your friends. This environment can have a negative or positive effect on how you feel about yourself and the character traits you develop. There are many factors that can contribute to the degree and form of your social anxiety.

Family Patterns

In studies, many shy people report that their parents have a controlling nature. If your parents are overprotective and don't allow you to make your own mistakes, you might begin to feel that you are not able to handle certain situations on your own. You may lack the self-confidence that is needed to be comfortable alone in a crowd. This could result in the fear of making mistakes and the fear of how others judge you.

Also, if your parents are socially anxious, you may have learned some of your behavior from watching them. Athene realizes that she developed many of her habits by reacting in ways similar to her mother.

> When I was younger, I always watched my mother get ready to go to parties and events. She would try on at least four outfits and never felt any of them were right. She quizzed my dad on who was going to be there and ordered him not to leave her side. I find myself doing the same things. I am always nervous about my appearance, even around close friends. I hate being left alone in a situation where I don't know very many people. I think we both have social anxiety.

Before you blame your parents for making you shy, remember that there are many factors at work. Perhaps you were already shy at a very young age and your parents were protective because you were anxious and easily upset. This may have led to a complicated pattern in which their desire to help you actually made you less confident of your own abilities. Also, remember that because of genetic factors, your parents may also have social anxiety. This would hinder their ability to help you overcome your own shyness.

No one is to blame for social anxiety. Neither you nor your parents are at fault. The most important thing is to understand the condition and learn ways to cope with it.

Learning from Negative Experiences

Many people with social anxiety can remember certain events that contributed to their fears. Martin knows exactly why he is afraid to speak in class.

> When I was in seventh-grade science class, the teacher had each student read aloud a paragraph from the textbook. It was a chapter on different types of organisms. When it was my turn, I accidentally said "orgasm" instead of "organism." Everyone howled with laughter, including the teacher. I felt so embarrassed. My face was bright red and I wanted to hide. Kids teased me about it for a long time. Ever since then, I am terrified about reading anything aloud. Sometimes, I am even afraid of simply speaking.

This event, together with Martin's biochemistry and genes, set him up to have a form of social anxiety. People who don't have the same heightened sense of awareness or the same chemicals rushing through their bodies may not have been upset by this event. They may have laughed with the class or even have been able to make fun of themselves.

Learning from Incorrect Information

The messages that society sends you are not always accurate. Females often hear that they should be kind, gentle, and sweet, whereas boys learn that they should be tough, strong, and unemotional. These messages can create much self-doubt and low self-esteem when someone doesn't measure up to the ideal. Often, as a result, he or she develops social anxiety.

>   *Joella has two older brothers. When she was younger, she loved to ride her bike, climb trees, and play baseball with them. Because there were no other kids in the neighborhood, they usually let her tag along. When she entered fifth grade, however, her best friend told her that none of the boys would ever like her because she acted like a tomboy. She showed Joella a magazine article that stated that a girl should let boys feel smarter and make them feel more powerful by acting helpless.*
>
>   *Even though it didn't feel right to her, Joella started trying to be "girly." But she couldn't help hitting the ball farther and running faster than most boys; and she wanted to do well in the science fair even though she remembered the article advised girls not to.*
>
>   *As a result of this conflict, Joella felt very unlikable. When she acted flirty and silly with the other girls, she felt false; but when she played baseball with the boys, she felt like she would never be feminine. She never knew how she should act. Soon, she became anxious in social situations and stopped playing baseball and going out with her female friends.*

Sociological Explanations

Sociologists theorize that people can live together in peace because of the development of a social hierarchy that ranges from dominant to submissive. Everyone in a group takes his or her place in the hierarchy. A certain degree of anxiety around others allows people to assess the level of threat that they pose, and helps maintain the balance between aggression and inhibition.

However, people with social anxiety tend to misinterpret others' behavior as more aggressive or powerful than it really is. As a result, a socially anxious person often will become overly submissive—blushing, not making eye contact, freezing, or withdrawing.

Sociologists believe this response may be the result of a fundamental fear of rejection. In monkeys, apes, and humans, being left to fend for oneself usually is a threat to survival. In social anxiety, people may see being judged as a threat to their position in the group. To them, rejection means failure.

Kyoto went through her day at school constantly apologizing to everyone. Whenever she walked down the hall, opened her locker, sat down in an empty seat, or got in line in the cafeteria, she always said "Excuse me" or "I'm sorry." Most of the time, she didn't know why she was apologizing. She always wanted to please others.

Kyoto's mother took her to see a psychologist because of Kyoto's anxiety. The psychologist helped Kyoto see that she misinterpreted others' behavior as being more aggressive than it was. Her constant need to apologize was meant to tell others, "I'm not a threat." Now, before she apologizes, Kyoto asks herself if it is really necessary. Usually, she finds that other people aren't angry at all.

How Life Is Affected
by Social Anxiety

Because you are reading this book, you probably know that social anxiety has a large impact on your life. It creates problems in school, at work, and in your social life. It hurts your relationships with your classmates, teachers, family, friends, and coworkers. Social anxiety also makes it hard to have fulfilling friendships. You probably find it difficult to meet new people and may feel as though you aren't very close to the friends you do have.

You may think that social anxiety will improve once you graduate from high school, go to college, or get a full-time job. Unfortunately, in most cases, a change in circumstances will not change your social anxiety. A study done by developmental psychologists shows that decisions made by socially anxious teens set patterns for the rest of their lives. Adolescents who are reluctant to enter social situations will have difficulty with the activities required to become spouses, parents, and members of the working world.

This chapter investigates the ways in which social anxiety may affect your life, now and in the future.

Problems in School

School may have been the first place where you confronted your social anxiety. When you entered school, it was probably the first time you were surrounded by strangers and were being evaluated on your abilities. As you grew older, the coursework became more difficult, and the evaluations became more important.

As you enter adolescence, the time when it is common to develop social anxiety, peer evaluation also becomes heightened. Suddenly, your classmates are noticing how you look, what you wear, what activities you participate in, and who your friends are. If you are shy, it can be difficult to feel good about yourself during this time.

Grades

Class participation is usually a big part of a final grade, and many people with social anxiety are afraid of speaking aloud. You may also be afraid of taking tests or you may suffer from writer's block. It can be very frustrating to know the answer to a question but be too anxious to raise your hand.

Sometimes, social anxiety in school is mistaken for apathy. If you never raise your hand in class or if you leave test questions blank, your teachers may assume you don't care about grades and that you aren't trying. It may be helpful to speak to your teachers and explain the problems you are having. They may be willing to help you work on your anxiety, perhaps by giving you more time to complete tests or by encouraging you to speak aloud during class.

If you don't try to improve your performance, these problems will haunt you for a long time. As we will see in the next section, the fear of speaking in front of others and being evaluated on your work makes it difficult to succeed after high school.

Fear of Trying New Things

High school is a time to figure out your interests. There are many clubs and groups that cover a wide variety of subjects. If you have social anxiety, however, you may be afraid of trying new things.

As we read earlier, many people with social anxiety are perfectionists. When you try something new, there is always a possibility that you won't be good at it. It is much safer to stick with what you know and avoid the possibility that you might fail or embarrass yourself in front of others.

In the future, however, you may regret not taking part in more activities. You may be upset that you did not take advantage of opportunities. Avoiding new activities now creates a pattern of avoidance that can be difficult to break.

Class Schedule

Social anxiety may also determine the classes you take. You may want to try something different, such as creative writing or shop, but you may be too afraid of what others will think and how they will judge what you produce. You may also be too intimidated by advanced classes to push yourself. Very smart people with social anxiety often stay with general courses to avoid a subject they may not understand.

Students suffering from social anxiety commonly avoid teachers who are known to pick on quiet students. Others might try to get teachers who always lecture, or only take large classes so they are less noticeable.

When you are in college, a reluctance to take new or challenging courses may make your academic career difficult. Most schools require students to take classes on a wide variety of subjects. A foreign language and difficult upper-level classes in your major will also be needed to graduate. You will need to venture out of your safety zone to fulfill such requirements.

Fear of Asking for Help

If you have social anxiety, it is probably very difficult to ask a teacher or classmate for help. Asking for help draws attention to yourself and makes you appear less than perfect.

At the beginning of the semester, Juan didn't understand a concept in his algebra class. Everyone else seemed to get it, so he didn't ask any questions. He was also too afraid to ask the teacher for help after class. He didn't want to bother her or make her angry. The course material for the next two weeks built on that same concept. Juan fell farther and farther behind in his homework and failed every quiz. He felt terrible and told himself he was stupid, which made the problem even more difficult.

If Juan had asked the teacher to explain the concept again, he wouldn't have gotten into this situation. Most teachers are willing to go over difficult material several times to make sure everyone understands. If you don't comprehend something, it may be that the teacher didn't explain it clearly.

Most schools have tutors or advisers available to help students. Taking advantage of such resources does not mean you are stupid. On the contrary, it means you are smart enough to realize when you need extra help.

Avoiding School or Dropping Out

Unfortunately, school sometimes becomes so difficult for people with social anxiety that they start avoiding it as much as they can. This has a serious effect on a person's future. It is difficult to get a good job with a decent salary if you do not have a high school diploma. If you drop out, you are setting yourself up for a difficult life.

Cedric has always had a hard time in school because of his extreme social anxiety. He feels uncomfortable with his classmates and avoids speaking with them. During classes, he always sits in the back and never participates. When teachers call on him, he usually mumbles "I don't know." As a result of his social anxiety, he has low self-esteem and suffers from depression.

One day, he decided that it didn't matter if he went to school or not. Some mornings, he hides in the yard until his mother leaves for work, and then he stays in his room all day. Other times, he wanders around the woods.

Cedric has no idea what he wants to do with his life. He knows it is only a matter of time before his mother finds out he has been missing school. He wishes he could just hide and hibernate. Deep down, he knows he has a problem, but he doesn't know what to do about it. Secretly, he hopes his mother forces him to see a therapist because he is afraid of what the rest of his life is going to be like.

Problems in the Workplace

This section shows how the problems you have in school carry over into the workplace. If you have a part-time job, you may already experience some of the following problems. If so, you should feel good that you are working on solving them now. They probably will not get better on their own.

Many people who have suffered from social anxiety for years finally ask for help when they recognize that their careers are suffering. They realize that they will never reach the level of success they want if they do not overcome their social fears.

Choosing Careers

Many people with social anxiety do not have the job they would like the most because of fear. They hold jobs in which their duties are clear and repetitive. They let other people make decisions because they do not want to be responsible. Social anxiety often causes people to find careers in which they can work alone. Many women with social anxiety immerse themselves in family to avoid the workplace altogether.

People suffering from social anxiety often remain at the same position for a long time because they are not seen as leaders. They avoid managerial roles and usually have a hard time communicating. As a result, work becomes boring, uninspired, and unfulfilling.

Debra has worked at the Boston Public Library for five years, returning books to the shelves. It is a very peaceful job and the only time she has to speak with people is when they ask her where to find certain books. She has always been a big reader, and the job seems like the perfect fit.

Lately, however, she has been feeling dissatisfied with her life. The library job doesn't pay very much so she still lives with her parents, at age twenty-seven. Most people she went to school with have exciting jobs and are getting married. Often, Debra feels like life is passing her by.

However, when she thinks about applying for a new job, Debra becomes very anxious. She is embarrassed that she has limited work experience and fears people will not take her seriously. She reads the Help Wanted section of the paper every day but is too scared to call for more information or to send out her résumé.

Inability to Promote Yourself

To be successful in the workplace, you need to be able to promote yourself. You need to demonstrate that you can handle more responsibility and challenging assignments. For people with social anxiety, this is difficult. Many times, they don't take credit for their ideas and don't volunteer for important projects. They stay in the shadows and try not to draw attention to themselves.

Another aspect of self-promotion is being able to communicate with your boss. Because many people with social anxiety have a hard time speaking with people in positions of authority, they are unable to have good relationships with their supervisors. As a result, they don't get promoted and may receive negative job evaluations. This has an effect on self-esteem and self-confidence, which compounds the problems caused by anxiety.

Inability to Connect with Coworkers

Full-time workers spend more time with coworkers than anyone else. Work is a much more enjoyable place if you have friends and healthy work relationships. If you feel anxious, this is difficult.

Coworkers are also a good source of information. If you are confused about an assignment, chances are someone else has been in that same situation and would be able to give you good advice. Talking with coworkers may lead to new ideas or improved efficiency.

Every morning, the people at Matthew's office congregate around the coffee pot and chat before the day begins. Matthew also likes to start the day with a cup of coffee so he usually goes to the break room, but he never speaks to anyone.

He is really envious of the easy way in which his colleagues speak with each other. He wishes he could be that open with people. Work is really lonely for him and he often watches the clock, counting the hours until he can go home and relax.

Bad Job Performance

Parts of your daily job may be very difficult if you have social anxiety, such as answering phones, chatting with customers, calling strangers, giving presentations, and being evaluated. If you are unable to perform these tasks well, you may be given fewer responsibilities, you may be demoted, or even fired.

Due to anxiety, you might begin to avoid work. You might be consistently late, take long lunches, or debate calling in sick every day. Responsibility and reliability are two traits that are very important to employers. If your social anxiety keeps you from being responsible and reliable, you will have a hard time keeping good jobs and getting positive recommendations from former bosses.

Problems in Your Social Life

Social anxiety can make you feel empty and alone. You may feel as though you go through each day like a robot— simply doing only what you need to without drawing attention to yourself. You may feel trapped in an unfulfilling and unsatisfying life.

When you suffer from anxiety, it is difficult to have the courage to change your situation. However, trying to get through life without the support of others is tough. The longer you live without creating fulfilling relationships, the more difficult it will be to make them in the future.

Loneliness

A recent study showed that 13.5 percent of college students are severely lonely. Overall, they felt that they were to blame for their loneliness. Characteristics of social anxiety, such as shyness, fear of rejection, and lack of social knowledge and experience, often were listed as reasons.

Loneliness is not the same thing as being alone. Many people enjoy solitude and find it a good time to be creative. They use time alone to write, read, listen to music, work on a hobby, or exercise. Often, sensitive people feel recharged after spending time alone. They make private time part of their schedules.

Loneliness is a problem when you find it unpleasant and distressing. Social bonds are considered necessary to psychological well-being. When it is difficult to develop and maintain relationships, you may find yourself vulnerable to increased stress, depression, other emotional disorders, and impaired physical health.

Inability to Be Close to People

Most people dream of having best friends with whom they share everything that they think and feel. For people with social anxiety, this dream rarely becomes reality. The openness and ability to trust that are necessary elements of friendship are difficult when you are afraid of being judged.

Melinda has a group of friends that she goes out with once in a while. Because Melinda looks older than she is and can use her sister's ID, her friends usually ask her to buy the alcohol. Melinda doesn't mind because once she has a beer or two, she loosens up and can talk and laugh with the other girls.

Sometimes, though, Melinda feels as though her friends use her only to buy alcohol. They never talk about anything serious and they don't know anything about her life. She longs for true friends who will share their lives and help each other through difficult times. She is too afraid to try to start new friendships, though. She fears that people will reject her. As a result, she keeps going out with the same crowd.

Fear of Dating

Dating is a big part of the teenage years. Dances, parties, and other social events can make you long for a significant other. However, if you have social anxiety, you may be terrified of getting close to someone of the opposite

53

sex. You may be afraid of saying something silly or acting inappropriately. Flirting, a playful way of getting noticed and letting someone know you like him or her, may seem impossible when you feel awkward and insecure.

If you are homosexual, the problems of dating are even more complex. Although dating between people of the opposite sex is accepted and encouraged, gay and lesbian teenagers often do not have the support of their friends, family, and community. Fighting that issue as well as dealing with social anxiety may make it seem as though you are destined to spend a lifetime alone.

Overcoming Social Anxiety

You may have recognized yourself in some of the descriptions of how social anxiety affects a person's life. You may have realized also how the problems associated with the condition can affect your life in the future. Now, you may be ready to try to overcome your social fears. The following chapters will show you ways to get started. If you make an effort, you will soon feel better about yourself and will be more comfortable in social situations.

Where to Start

Whether you have suffered from social anxiety for most of your life or for only a short time, the problems associated with it can seem impossible to overcome. Because social anxiety affects many parts of your life, you may not know where to start when learning to cope with it. This chapter teaches you two important techniques: journal writing and goal setting.

Once you begin practicing both of these techniques, the overwhelming problems of social anxiety will be more manageable. You will realize which issues you need to work on most and will discover methods to help you move forward.

Journal Writing

Keeping a journal is an extremely valuable practice. Right now, your mind may be racing with anxious thoughts and worries. Writing them down helps you sort through your problems and come to a deeper understanding of the issues in your life.

The benefits of journal writing may be more than just psychological. Dr. James Pennebaker, a researcher in Texas, discovered that when people write about difficult experiences for twenty minutes at a time over a period of three to four days, their immune system functioning increases. This indicates that the simple act of writing about emotions has a direct impact on your body's ability to withstand stress and fight infection and disease.

How Journal Writing Helps

Because of your social anxiety, you may be so afraid that any opinions you have are wrong that you remain neutral on most subjects. Or, you might feel like a chameleon who changes opinions depending on the situation. Not expressing your opinions can make you feel empty and unsure of what you really believe. Writing your thoughts and feelings in a journal can help you figure out your likes and dislikes, your opinions on tough issues, and what you stand for. Once you have your true beliefs down on paper, they will seem more concrete and you will be able to remember them during social situations.

Although you probably are aware of what causes you the most anxiety, you also may have worries that are more difficult to identify. People often use various mental tricks to bury problems that are painful or difficult. As you write in your journal, you will become more aware of hidden fears and worries. Once they are brought into the open, you can begin to cope with them more effectively.

Writing about events also makes it easier to be objective. While a belief, such as "Everyone thinks I'm stupid," may cross your mind unconsciously, writing it down makes you realize how false and exaggerated it is. Once you see how maladaptive some of your thoughts are, it is easier to change them.

In addition, a journal is valuable whenever you feel discouraged. Reviewing past entries will remind you how much you have improved over time. This insight will help you stay motivated and will make you want to keep working on the problem. Past entries are also helpful in figuring out how to deal with events in the present. You can look back at various situations, discover what actions worked (or didn't), and feel confident in repeating them (or not).

Possible Problems with Journal Writing

Be careful not to get too involved with your journal. In many published journals, writers such as Anäis Nin worried that they found writing in a journal so satisfying that they were trapped into spending their lives writing about events, rather than living them. Don't let writing about feelings replace speaking with others. Journal writing should be a tool to help you become more confident, not a crutch that increases your isolation. If you find yourself becoming too dependent on your journal, take a break from writing for a week or two.

Writing on Paper

A benefit of writing in a paper journal is that the only limitation is the size of the page. Be creative and make the book a reflection of your personality. Besides writing, you can draw or paint, glue in mementos like ticket stubs or photos, use different-colored pens and pencils, and insert letters and notes. You can write sideways or upside down on the page, and doodle in the margins. Writing in the journal can be fun. Your journal can be an expression of your individuality.

Journaling Tips

- Try to write every day. Set aside a special time—perhaps right before you go to bed—to reflect on what happened during that day. Writing things down soon after they happen will help you to be honest and objective. If you wait, you may not remember the details as well, and maladaptive thinking patterns may cloud your interpretations.

- Record the date and time for every entry. Also, give each entry a title that reflects what you wrote about. This will help when you search for old entries about a particular day or topic.

- Don't worry about spelling, grammar, punctuation, or organization. Being a perfectionist will lead to frustration. You aren't going to be graded on your journal—just write whatever comes to mind.

- Leave blank space for future comments. Reflecting on entries weeks, months, or even years after you wrote them will help you record your progress.

- Keep the journal in a safe place. Journal writing is most effective when you are completely honest. This may be hard if you are afraid your parents or siblings might read it.

Using the Computer

If you spend a lot of time on a computer, this format may seem more natural than writing by hand in a book. There are many advantages to using a computer.

One advantage is increased legibility. It may be easier to look back when the entries are typed. Can you type faster than you can write? If so, you might find it frustrating to write by hand when you are used to the speed of typing.

Keeping records of your progress on a computer is also very easy. A table or electronic spreadsheet is an effective way to record information in a clear, easy-to-read format. Analyzing the information by using the various sorting mechanisms makes it possible to figure out patterns of behavior or common situations in which you feel anxiety.

Online Journals

There are many Web sites devoted to writing journals online. Before beginning an online journal, there are several things you should check. The first is the privacy of your journal. Some Web sites post people's entries for others to view, while other sites let you choose to keep them private. Whether or not to show your journal to the public is a personal decision. On one hand, privacy may increase your honesty. On the other hand, allowing others to read and comment on your thoughts may help you overcome your fear of judgment.

Lucas laughed when he first heard that journal writing helped improve social anxiety. He thought about the little pink diary his sister had hidden under her bed. He logged on to one of the free online journal services and decided to write for a few days, anyway.

The first day he wrote about the moments that he felt anxious—where and when it happened, why he thought he was stressed, and what his thoughts and feelings were at the time. The next day he continued to record times of anxiety but also wrote about what he wanted to change about himself and why. The third day he wrote a few goals and the steps he could take to achieve them.

He was amazed by how much better he felt after only three days. Writing about his worries seemed to clear his mind. Because other people could read his goals and desires on the Web site, he felt motivated to accomplish them. Also, several people commented that his postings helped them to confront their own social fears.

Ideas for Journal Entries

You may find the following ideas useful in beginning your journal or keeping the entries varied. If you are not used to expressing your thoughts on paper, it may seem awkward at first. The longer you do it, the easier it will become. You'll be amazed at the insight you gain into your life.

⮑ Write about your most memorable experience with social anxiety. How did you feel? What did you think? How did others react? Why do you think the event happened?

⮑ Write about situations that make you anxious every day. Record your thoughts, feelings, and actions. You may want to divide the page into columns with the headings: situation or event; negative thoughts; physical reactions; and actions. Following is an example of how this may look:

Situation or Event	Negative Thoughts	Physical Reactions	Actions
Should I attend the first art class after school.	I thought about skipping out. I was afraid of what people would think. I wanted to do a good job.	I felt a shortness of breath. In general, I was nervous and in a bad mood.	I took some deep breaths and visualized the class going well. Later, I became engrossed in my drawing.

↬ Write about a time when you were pleased with how you acted in a social situation.

↬ Identify times when anxiety symptoms kept you from doing something that you really wanted to do. How did you feel? What might have happened if you had not been afraid?

↬ Write a letter to someone who made you feel bad about yourself. You aren't going to show the letter to anyone, so feel free to write whatever you want.

↬ Write out a conversation with your inner voice. Begin the entry with a question directed to yourself, then write your mental response. It may help to label the different voices *A* and *B*. Dialogue writing is a very effective way to get to the heart of the matter.

The following passage is an example of typical dialogue writing:

A: Tomorrow is a big day. You have an interview at a college. How do you feel?

B: I am really nervous. This is the first interview and I don't know what it is going to be like.

A: What are you afraid of?

B: I'm afraid I'll stutter and say something stupid. I'm worried the person will ask a question and I won't know what to say.

A: What do you want to discuss?

B: I think it is good that I was on the basketball team for four years. That shows commitment and dedication. I also got decent grades and earned a blue ribbon at the science fair.

A: What about your hobbies outside of school?

B: I really like to read. I could mention that. I could talk also about the vacations my family has taken. They are pretty interesting. I enjoy my part-time retail job.

A: It sounds like you do a lot.

B: I guess I am good at organizing my life and

accomplishing what needs to be done. Hey, that would sound good in an interview!

↪ Try focused "freewriting." Pick one topic, such as school, friends, or family, and write everything that comes to mind about that topic. Write for at least ten minutes or until you're certain that you have run out of things to write.

↪ Write your belief system. Start by writing "I believe..." at the top of a clean page. Then write whatever comes to mind. It may help to ask yourself questions when you get stuck such as "What do I believe about friendship?" "What is my personal style?" or "What are my gifts and abilities?"

↪ Write about an event from your perspective, then write about the same event from someone else's point of view. For example, if you had a hard time answering a question during class, write about how you felt, what you thought, and how you behaved. Next, pretend you are the teacher writing about the same event. What do you think he or she was thinking? How did he or she act? This exercise is a great way to show that there are multiple ways of seeing the same situation.

Goal Setting

Another powerful method to tackle social anxiety is to develop goals and objectives. Goal setting allows you to determine where you want to go in life instead of passively allowing events to direct your path. Research has shown that people who develop goals throughout their lives suffer less from stress, perform better, and show more self-confidence. Goal setting gives you the long-term vision and short-term motivation to develop the skills you need to succeed.

Five Elements of a Good Goal

There are five elements of a useful goal. The first is that it is specific—you should describe what you want to accomplish with as much detail as possible. "I want to get rid of social anxiety" is not a good goal; it is too broad and general. Instead, pick a specific symptom or situation to improve. A useful goal might be, "I want to feel confident when I meet new people." You also should express the goal positively. For example, "Make a useful and challenging goal" is much more effective than "Don't make a stupid goal."

The second element is that the goal should be performance-oriented, not outcome-oriented. You should have as much control over your goal as possible. If things beyond your control, such as weather, injury, or others' opinions, can have an effect on whether or not you achieve your goal, you need to rethink it. For example, if your goal is to win first place at a speech competition and you come in third, you probably will see this as a failure, even if you gave the best speech you ever have. If you set performance goals, such as not forgetting lines, remembering to make eye contact with the judges, and using voice inflections, you will have achieved the goal independently of the other speakers' performances and the judges' opinions.

The third element is to make the goal challenging. It should take energy and discipline to accomplish the task.

You may be setting the goals too low if you are frightened of failure. Remember that failure is not a bad thing—it highlights what you need to work on, and where you can improve your skills and abilities. Setting your goals too low is often an excuse to avoid difficult tasks. If you aren't ready to push yourself and work hard, then it is unlikely that you will improve your social anxiety.

The fourth element of a good goal is that it is realistic. It should be out of your immediate reach, but not so far that there is no hope of achieving it. You won't put a serious effort into goals that you know are impossible. Creating goals such as "I want to be the center of attention at parties" or "I never want to be nervous again" will only lead to disappointment and frustration.

The last element is that you think the goal through completely. When you make a goal, you want to have a clear path for achieving it. It shouldn't be some abstract ideal held far in the future. To get a good sense of the goal, ask yourself the following questions:

➯ What skills do I need to meet this goal?

➯ Do I need outside help to meet this goal?

➯ What can block my progress?

➯ Am I making any false assumptions?

It is easy to base your goals on what other people, such as your parents, teachers, or friends, want for you. Often, this is in conflict with your own goals, desires, and ambitions. Use your journal to help determine what your dreams for the future are, and to make goals that help you achieve them.

During high school, Jonah's main goal was to become a doctor. He studied well and got good grades so he could go to a top college. His father and his grandfather were both doctors, and they often talked about how wonderful it would be to have three generations of doctors in the family.

Once he got to college, Jonah found that he wasn't as interested in biology and chemistry as he was in his literature and writing classes. He joined the school newspaper and often spent evenings writing stories for its front page instead of studying for his pre-med classes. Finally, he realized that becoming a doctor was his family's goal, not his. He wanted to become a journalist instead.

Prioritize Your Goals

You probably have many goals covering a wide range of areas. It can be overwhelming to think about working on so much at one time. This is why it is important to prioritize your goals.

Think about what is most important to you. It may be your relationships with your family or friends, your grades, or participation in an extracurricular activity. Once you have prioritized the issues in your life, it will become easier to see which of your goals is the most important.

Develop Long-Term and Short-Term Goals

You should have both long-term and short-term goals in mind. Long-term goals take a great deal of time to accomplish—sometimes years. Short-term goals can be achieved relatively quickly and are often used as steps to help reach the other, long-term goals.

Perhaps your long-term goal is to have more meaningful relationships with people. Because this goal isn't concrete and there is no tangible way to know when you achieve it, it should be coupled with short-term goals. Examples of short-term goals might be to invite a friend out for pizza with you, to have good conversations with people at a social gathering, to make small talk with people each week between classes, or to open up about your feelings with a few friends or family members.

Determine an Action Plan

Once you have developed and prioritized your long-term and short-term goals, it is necessary to think of an action plan. An action plan is a list of specific steps that will help you attain your goals. Try to make the elements of your action plan part of your daily life. In this way you will be more aware of your progress. You can add to your action plan as you realize issues on which you need to keep working.

Let's look at some people's situations, the long- and short-term goals they developed, and the specific steps they planned to take to achieve their goals.

Curt knows he has to give a presentation in biology class. It is an important presentation that counts as 40 percent of his grade. So far, Curt has done well in the class, but he is terrified that his presentation will lower his overall grade. He is putting great pressure on himself to do a good job and feels extremely anxious. He is certain that he will forget lines, that the teacher will ask him a question he can't answer, and that he will stutter.

Curt's long-term goal: I want to feel confident about my abilities to speak in public.

Curt's short-term goal: I want to feel calm when I give my presentation in front of the class.

Curt's Action Steps:

- ⇀ I will spend three weeks preparing so I will feel good about my material.

- ⇀ I will practice giving the speech—first by myself, then with my family as the audience.

- ⇀ I will write out the speech on note cards so I won't have to worry about forgetting lines.

- ⇀ The night before the speech, I will visualize myself performing well. I will visualize the class and teacher having a positive response.

Lisa has a group of friends she goes out with regularly. However, she feels uncomfortable and out of place with them. She often thinks that they ask her to go along just because she is there when the plans are being made. When they go out, Lisa is very quiet. When she does speak, it is usually a simple response to something someone else says; she rarely gives her own opinion.

Lisa's long-term goal: I want to feel comfortable expressing my thoughts and feelings to others.

Lisa's short-term goal: When I go out with friends, I want to feel more relaxed.

Lisa's Action Steps:

> ➷ I will suggest things to do instead of just going along with what other people decide.
>
> ➷ I will call the friends I want to get to know better and speak with them outside of the group so I feel more comfortable with them in the group.
>
> ➷ I will think of three topics of conversation to introduce during the evening, such as current movies, class assignments, or an upcoming holiday or social event.

Now, using the guidelines in this chapter, think about what your goals are and how you plan to achieve them. Write your goals and action plans in your journal. Studies have shown that when goals are written down, people have a much better chance of achieving them. When goals exist only in your mind, they usually aren't specific enough.

In the next chapters we will explore some additional techniques to help you cope with social anxiety as you work toward accomplishing your goals.

How to
Help Yourself Cope

As we discussed in chapter 2, there are three ways in which anxiety affects people: physically, mentally, and behaviorally. In this section, you will learn techniques to help yourself cope with these various responses to your fear of social situations.

At first, practice the techniques when you are alone, perhaps in the privacy of your bedroom. Then, once you become familiar with them, you can begin to use them in social situations. If you practice the techniques enough, you will be able to incorporate them into your everyday life.

People with social anxiety tend to put a lot of pressure on themselves to act perfectly. It is important that you don't expect to perform these techniques flawlessly. They are skills that need to be developed and practiced. Remember that it takes time to learn new things. Be patient. The first few times you try these techniques, the goal should be simply to feel a little better than when you started.

You may have all sorts of thoughts running through your head while trying these techniques, such as "I don't feel completely relaxed. There's something wrong with me." Thoughts about events that you fear may also creep into your mind, such as, "I have to go to that party tonight. What am I going to wear? What if no one talks to me?" Try to push those thoughts away. For some people, it helps to imagine throwing those worries in a garbage can or locking them in a closet. If you can focus entirely on the activity, it will be more beneficial.

Easing Your Body's Response to Anxiety

As explained earlier, anxiety has a strong impact on your body. When you feel anxious, your heart races, breathing becomes difficult, your face gets red, and you tremble. When your body deals with anxiety over long periods of time, you may develop stomachaches, headaches, depression, and sore muscles.

To combat these negative effects, you need to learn how to relax physically. Once your muscles relax, then the other components of a relaxed state follow: Your breathing pattern slows and deepens, your heart rate and blood pressure decline, your hands and feet feel warm, changes in mood occur, and you feel calmer.

There are many ways to relax your body. Some techniques focus on your muscles. Others center on breathing patterns. Relaxation techniques are most beneficial if you practice them on a regular basis. Your body must have these responses "memorized" for them to be helpful in a time of anxiety. We will look at several techniques in this section.

Progressive Muscle Relaxation

Even when you feel at ease, you may still experience tightness in your body. People with chronic anxiety often have a hard time telling when their muscles are completely relaxed because feeling tense is their natural state.

Progressive muscle relaxation (PMR) is a two-step technique that helps you recognize when your muscles are tense and when they are relaxed. First, you deliberately tense certain muscle groups. Second, you release the tension and become aware of how the relaxed muscles feel.

It is recommended that you practice PMR every day in a quiet place with no distractions until you feel capable of performing the practice in social situations. Ultimately, you will be able to use PMR whenever you feel any anxiety.

How to Perform Progressive Muscle Relaxation

Make sure you are wearing loose clothing and that you remove your shoes. Sit in a comfortable chair with your body fully supported.

First, tense all the muscles in the area you are targeting. Concentrate on how tight they feel. Next, relax the muscles that were just tensed. Imagine they have turned to jelly and concentrate on how limp and loose they feel. When that muscle group is completely relaxed, move on to the next area. It is recommended that you work all the major muscle groups in your body, listed as follows. When you have finished, keep your eyes closed for a few seconds, then get up slowly.

➭ Right foot

➭ Right calf and foot

⮑ Entire right leg

⮑ Left foot

⮑ Left calf and foot

⮑ Entire left leg

⮑ Right hand

⮑ Right forearm and hand

⮑ Entire right arm

⮑ Left hand

⮑ Left forearm and hand

⮑ Entire left arm

⮑ Face

⮑ Neck and shoulders

⮑ Abdomen

⮑ Chest

Paced Breathing

People who experience anxiety often breathe improperly. They take shallow breaths from their chests instead of deep breaths from their diaphragms. (The diaphragm is the muscle that separates your chest cavity from your abdominal cavity and that makes it possible for you to inhale and exhale.)

Breathing from the chest can cause you to hyperventilate, which has a negative effect on your body's chemistry.

Hyperventilation does not only mean panting or gasping for air; it also includes yawning, holding your breath, and sighing. The symptoms of hyperventilation are similar to those associated with anxiety: shortness of breath, light-headedness, faintness, tingling or numbness in your fingers and toes, and the feeling that you are walking around in a dream. If you deal with anxiety and begin to hyperventilate, it will make the situation even worse.

How to Perform Paced Breathing

Paced breathing is a slow, regular rate of deep breathing. There are three main points to keep in mind when practicing:

1. Breathe slowly. Concentrate on slowing the rate of your breathing to eight or ten breaths per minute.

2. Inhale and exhale through your nose. It is more difficult to take shallow breaths from the upper chest when you breathe through your nose. This keeps you from hyperventilating.

3. Choose a neutral word to focus on while practicing paced breathing. The words "one," "calm," and "relax" work well. Each time you exhale, say the word in your mind. This will assist in keeping your breathing evenly paced, and will help to reduce the chances of interfering thoughts.

During the day, when you are not practicing paced breathing, alternate paced and normal breathing. Every single breath you take does not have to come from the diaphragm. There should be a natural rhythm between chest breathing and diaphragm breathing. Find a

comfortable balance but do more diaphragmatic breathing than you usually do.

> *Tony is at a local law office to interview for an
> internship. He wants to become a trial lawyer. He is
> very excited by the thought of working professionally,
> but is so anxious about the interview that he feels
> lightheaded and numb. He is afraid he won't be able
> to say what he wants to, and that his answers will
> be incorrect.*
> *As he waits for the interviewer, Tony starts to con-
> centrate on slowing the rate of his breathing. With only
> a few deep breaths, his mind clears and his racing
> heart calms. He feels more relaxed and is confident.*

Autogenic Training

Autogenic training has been a very effective technique for
stress reduction and relaxation since the neuropsychologist
J. W. Schultz created it in 1932. Schultz recognized that
people experience feelings of heaviness and warmth during
hypnosis. He developed autogenic training so they could
recreate this relaxed state, thereby reducing tension.

How to Practice Autogenic Training

As in PMR, you should practice autogenic training in a
quiet, dark place. Sit comfortably and wear loose clothing.
As you become more experienced, you can incorporate this
technique into your daily life whenever you feel anxious.

The first step in autogenic training is to create a feeling
of heaviness in the specific body part you are focusing on,
for example, the right arm. Make your arm feel like it is
made out of lead as you say, "My right arm is very heavy"

to yourself six times. Next, create a feeling of warmth in the arm as you imagine the blood vessels relaxing and dilating. Say, "My right arm is very warm," six times. Continue with the left arm and both legs.

Next, concentrate on your heart rate. Say the phrase "My heart beats calmly and regularly" six times as you relax. Then, pay attention to your breathing. Every breath should be deep and should come from the diaphragm. Don't attempt to influence the rate of your breathing— instead allow it to determine its own rhythm as you repeat "My breathing is calm and regular" six times.

The next step is to calm your abdominal organs. Often, people with chronic anxiety suffer from constipation, indigestion, and similar disturbances; this step helps loosen any tension. Say the phrase "My abdomen is flowing warmly" six times. Next, imagine that your forehead is relieved of any tension while repeating the phrase "My forehead is pleasantly cool."

To complete the exercise, revive yourself by saying "Arms firm. Breathe deep. Open eyes." You should feel calm and relaxed, yet alert and refreshed.

Marisol started practicing autogenic training when her parents began planning her high school graduation party. Most of their relatives and friends were invited— the guest list had over eighty people on it.

At the party, she felt anxious when a group of her parents' friends began asking her what she planned to study in college. Because she had become so good at autogenic training, she simply said to herself, "My arms feel heavy and warm" to feel more comfortable and at ease.

Physical Exercise

Physical exercise is an excellent way to reduce tension. In the 1980s, it was discovered that exercise increases the amount of certain neurotransmitters that help the body deal with anxiety. Exercise also increases adrenaline levels, improves oxygen consumption and circulation, and stimulates the production of endorphins. In addition, the satisfaction that comes from knowing that you are healthy and fit will improve your self-esteem.

Unfortunately, many people view exercise as a chore. The best way to keep exercise exciting is to do a wide range of enjoyable activities. Five days a week of walking on a treadmill will be mind-numbing, but if you include other activities, such as dancing or riding your bike, it will be much more interesting.

Setting goals is also a good way to stay motivated. If you have begun to jog after school, train for a road race. If you walk or ride your bike, set a goal of reaching 100 miles. Think of exercise as a positive part of healthy living, not work.

Easing Your Mind's Responses to Anxiety

When you are in social situations, your mind might race with negative thoughts about yourself, expectations about what is going to happen, or fears about what others are thinking. Often, these thoughts develop into a vicious cycle: Because you believe you don't have anything worthwhile to express, you expect to have difficulty speaking. When you have difficulty speaking, you believe that people think you're stupid. Because you believe people think you are stupid, you have even more difficulties with conversation. With your mind in such a tizzy, it is difficult to relax and be yourself.

Your imagination is a very powerful tool to help combat negative self-talk and reduce stress, tension, and anxiety. This section will help you learn to think your way out of this mental trap.

Visualization

One way to calm your mind is to replace your maladaptive thoughts with a relaxing, happy scene. You probably can remember a place where the scenery completely relaxed you—maybe it was at the beach or in your backyard, lying in a hammock. In visualization, you focus on this calming memory.

How to Perform Visualization

To practice visualization, sit in a comfortable position and relax any muscle tension. Once you feel relaxed, begin to visualize a pleasant scene. Imagine every aspect of the scene, using all of your senses. For instance, if you visualize sitting on a beach watching the ocean waves lapping against the shore, imagine first what the scene looks like, then imagine how the sand feels on your bare feet. Take a deep breath and imagine how the clean ocean air smells and tastes. Next, listen for the sounds of the waves and seagulls.

As you become more involved with your mental picture, your body will relax and you will be able to let go of your worrisome thoughts. It often helps to make positive, affirmative statements, such as "I feel calm and relaxed," while practicing to block negative thoughts more effectively. You could picture also an image that represents the tension you feel when you begin, such as a kite that is stuck in a tree getting more and more tangled. As you become relaxed, imagine the string loosening and the kite becoming free and soaring in the sky.

With practice, you will be able to use this technique to help yourself relax whenever you feel distressed.

Lori spent last Thanksgiving at her best friend Haley's house. Most of the members of Haley's large, extended family were there. Everyone was talking at once, the children were running around, and Lori felt completely overwhelmed. It was so different from her quiet house.

As she felt herself getting more agitated and anxious, she went upstairs to the bathroom and began to visualize herself at her family's quiet cabin. She heard the wind rustling through the leaves and the chirping of birds. She smelled the soil and felt the coolness of the air. Soon, she felt calm and relaxed and was able to return downstairs.

Replace Maladaptive Thoughts with Coping Statements

When you feel anxious in social situations, you probably have many false beliefs and maladaptive thoughts, such as "I don't fit in" or "I'm so awkward." An important part of coping with social anxiety is to be able to recognize when your thinking is clouded.

Use your journal to record events that make you feel anxious, and examine what you were thinking at the time and why. It may help to refer to the list of maladaptive thinking patterns on pages 25 and 26 to help you see when your thinking is faulty. Remember that figuring out your faulty thoughts requires that you be totally honest with yourself. Once you have identified your maladaptive thoughts, you can work to replace them with more constructive thoughts, called coping statements.

How to Create Coping Statements

Coping statements should be brief and simple so you can easily remember them when you feel anxious. They should apply directly to the situation you fear—if you are worried about your hand shaking while you eat, a statement about public speaking won't help. They should also be realistic. You might try to counter anxious feelings with a statement like, "I won't be nervous." That statement is too unrealistic to help; everyone feels nervous at times. Your statements should help you cope with the nervousness. Some examples of effective coping statements include:

- Relax. I'm in control.

- My friends will still accept me if I say something silly.

- It's not that bad. I can do it.

You may want to write your coping statement on a piece of paper to carry with you. You can also write other helpful comments on it. Then, when you become anxious, you can read the coping card and can remind yourself that you can change the way you think. Often, simply having the card with you is calming whether you refer to it or not.

Change Your Inaccurate Expectations

Many social fears are caused by inaccurate expectations and "catastrophizing." One way to determine your expectations is to figure out exactly what you fear. For instance, if you are going to a friend's birthday party and you feel overly anxious, ask yourself "Why am I afraid?" "Because I am going to a party" isn't a good answer, because the party itself does not lead to anxiety. You need to determine what you expect will happen at the party to determine what is making you nervous. You might find that you believe no one will talk to you or that your friend will hate your gift. Once you identify concrete fears and expectations, you can work to change your maladaptive thinking patterns.

Changing Expectations by Estimating Probability

A step in correcting your inaccurate expectations is to figure out how likely it is that what you fear will occur. Here are four ways to estimate the probability of an event:

1. **Remember past experiences**. If you are afraid that no one will speak with you at the party, think about other parties you have attended. Have you ever been to a social gathering where no one spoke to you? Chances are that you probably have not.

2. **Look at general rules**. If you are worried about spilling something, look at your general experience with how people deal with spills. When someone else spilled, did everyone laugh and gossip about that person? Most likely, they didn't. Spills happen all the time, especially at parties where people are carrying food and drinks. The general rule about spills is that they are usually cleaned up quickly without much fuss.

3. **Think about alternate explanations**. What you expect is only one possibility. There are also many other possibilities for why something happens. For instance, if a friend from summer camp stops e-mailing you, you might think he or she has decided you are not a good friend. However, there are many other possibilities. He or she simply may be very busy or maybe he or she has forgotten that you wrote last.

4. **Practice role reversal**. This is one of the best methods for realizing how critical you are of yourself. Pretend that whatever you fear actually happens to someone else. For instance, if you are afraid your friend will hate your gift, imagine that he or she gives you a gift that you don't like. What would you think? Chances are you would be happy to have a friend who gives you gifts.

Using the Worst-Case Scenario Technique

Another way to correct inaccurate expectations is to imagine what would happen if the worst possible scenario occurred. Pretend that everything has gone wrong at once. Picture all the details and then exaggerate them. As you visualize the worst situation possible, you may start to laugh. The scene will seem so ridiculous that you realize there is not the slightest chance that it will take place.

Lupe used the worst-case scenario technique after deciding that she really wanted to join the yearbook committee. The students in the group met after school once a week, and Lupe felt anxious about attending her first meeting. She was certain she would clam up when people spoke to her. The morning before the meeting, she relaxed and imagined the worst things that could happen. She pictured herself saying something and everyone ignoring her. She pictured her face getting so red that it looked like she was going to explode. Then she imagined people laughing at her, saying she didn't belong.

This exercise helped Lupe realize that her fears were unfounded. That afternoon, after a little pep talk and a few deep breaths, Lupe walked into the meeting. She was relieved that people were genuinely happy to have her there. She felt proud that she was able to be involved in a situation that she would have previously avoided.

Acting in New Ways

Social anxiety also has a strong impact on how you act. As explained before, when people experience anxiety they usually either freeze or completely avoid the situation. These maladaptive coping mechanisms may protect you in the present, but will probably cause you to lose confidence and lower your self-esteem over time. The final part of coping with social anxiety is to practice new ways to behave.

Behavior Rehearsal

Behavior rehearsal is practicing your actions until you feel confident about them. The first step is to visualize the ideal situation. Imagine the scenario and see yourself feeling relaxed and comfortable. Imagine others reacting positively and think about what you will say and do. It may also help to write out the scenario in your journal. Sometimes writing down what you want to say "cements" it in your mind.

Next, practice what you imagined. It may help to do this with a friend or family member acting as the other characters. For instance, if you are afraid to call about a job opening, rehearse what you want to say with your mom or dad playing the role of the employer. Or, if you are going to an event where you do not know many people, practice with a sibling introducing yourself to a stranger.

Pay special attention to the various maladaptive thoughts and expectations you may have regarding the situation. Analyze them and explore how realistic they are. Once you feel you have a handle on the situation, develop a few coping statements for extra support.

Modeling

Modeling is the process of watching how others act in certain situations, then copying their behavior. For example, if you are worried about the first impression you make, pay attention to how others present themselves. What traits give a good first impression? What do people say? How do confident people carry themselves? Also examine people who give a bad first impression and try to determine why. Imitate the actions that impressed you. With time, you will feel more comfortable with modeling and begin to own the traits you admire in others.

Modeling works very well when you are in an unfamiliar situation. If you are not sure how to act, watching others will give you clues.

Sam's best friend's father passed away and Sam attended the service. He had never been to a funeral before and felt very uncomfortable. As he stood in the receiving line, he felt anxious about what to say and how to act. He was terrified of saying the wrong thing and hurting his friend's family.

Sam stepped out of line and stood to the side for a moment. He observed what other people did as he breathed deeply and practiced relaxation techniques. After a few minutes, he figured out what to do and returned to the line. When he reached his friend's mother, he gave her a hug and said, "I'm so sorry for your loss." She hugged him back and thanked him for coming. Sam felt confident that he had acted appropriately.

What If I Need More Help?

After trying the techniques in the previous chapter, you may still feel overwhelmed by social anxiety and may want the guidance of someone who has studied the disorder. If this is the case, you should consider seeking professional therapy.

You should get help immediately if you are feeling depressed and suicidal, or if you are considering acts of violence. Also, if you have been abusing drugs and/or alcohol to deal with your anxiety, you need outside help to overcome your addiction.

Therapy is conducted by trained professionals who are knowledgeable about psychological problems and who have access to research and recent developments in treatment. Seeing a therapist about social anxiety can be more beneficial than working through it on your own.

Unfortunately, many people in our society see therapy as a sign of weakness. That is not true. Recognizing the need to see a professional therapist is actually a sign of strength. It is a testament to your determination to live a happy, healthy life.

Types of Professionals

Physicians

Your family physician is a good person to approach about social anxiety. He or she is aware of your medical history and may know whether anxiety or depression runs in your family. Also, because you probably have seen him or her before, you may feel more comfortable speaking to him or her than speaking with a complete stranger.

Your physician is able to prescribe medication, but he or she is not trained as a psychologist. After the initial consultation, your physician may refer you to someone who is specially trained in mental disorders.

Psychologists and Psychiatrists
Psychologists and psychiatrists are trained therapists who help people cope with and solve their problems. The main difference between the two is that a psychiatrist is also a physician and can prescribe medication. Before you decide between a psychologist or psychiatrist, you should evaluate how you feel about taking medication for social anxiety. Types of drug treatments will be discussed later in this chapter.

Types of Degrees for Professionals
When you begin to investigate therapists, you will probably see a wide array of initials following their names. That alphabet soup indicates academic degrees, licenses, and/or certifications.

Remember that just because the professional has a lot of impressive degrees, that doesn't mean that he or she is the right therapist for you. The most important thing is to feel completely comfortable with the person so you can speak honestly about your feelings. If you are uncomfortable or intimidated, your time with the therapist will not be effective.

When finding a therapist, you should look for one with a master's degree or a doctorate in a mental-health field.

This shows that he or she has had advanced training in dealing with psychological problems. Therapists' academic degrees include:

M.D. (Doctor of Medicine): This means that the doctor received his or her medical degree and has had four years of clinical residency. M.D.s can prescribe medication.

Ph.D. (Doctor of Philosophy) and Psy.D. (Doctor of Psychology): These professionals have had four to six years of graduate study. They frequently work in businesses, schools, mental-health centers, and hospitals.

M.A. (Master of Arts degree in psychology): An M.A. is basically a counseling degree. Therapists with this degree emphasize clinical experience and psychotherapy.

M.S. (Master of Science degree in psychology): Professionals with this degree are more inclined toward research and usually have a specific area of focus.

Ed.D. (Doctor of Education): This degree indicates a background in education, child development, and general psychology.

M.S.W. (Master of Social Work): An M.S.W. is a social-work degree that prepares an individual to diagnose and treat psychological problems and provide mental health resources. Psychiatric social workers make up the single largest group of mental health professionals.

In additional to the various degrees therapists may hold, there are also a number of licenses that may be obtained. These include:

M.F.C.C.: Marriage, Family, and Child Counselor

M.F.T.: Marriage and Family Therapist

L.C.S.W.: Licensed Clinical Social Worker

L.I.S.W.: Licensed Independent Social Worker

L.S.W.: Licensed Social Worker

Types of Therapy

There are many types of therapy used to treat social anxiety. Each one has developed from a different theory about the causes of the disorder.

Classical Psychoanalytic Therapy

If you are unfamiliar with therapy, you may imagine that the patient lies on a couch while a psychologist asks probing questions about the patient's past. This is actually a very specific type of therapy, known as classical psychoanalysis. In general, classical psychoanalysis emphasizes the importance of discovering and resolving internal, unconscious conflicts, usually by exploring your childhood and past experiences. It was developed by Sigmund Freud in the 1890s, and it is much less popular now than it once was.

This type of therapy does not work very well for people with social anxiety. Although it may be useful for understanding behaviors associated with social anxiety, it doesn't teach ways of dealing with the problem.

Behavioral Therapy

Behavioral therapy differs dramatically from classical psychoanalysis. Instead of dealing with an individual's thoughts, feelings, and past experiences, it focuses solely on the specific behaviors that are causing problems. Behavioral therapists believe that all behaviors are learned and that you can relearn and replace maladaptive behaviors with more appropriate ones.

Cognitive Therapy

Instead of behavior, cognitive therapy emphasizes changing thoughts and beliefs. Cognitive therapists believe that irrational beliefs or distorted thinking patterns lead to social anxiety so they teach patients to think in more rational, constructive ways.

Cognitive-Behavioral Therapy

There are almost no pure cognitive or behavioral therapists. Instead, most therapists use a combination of both techniques. This is known as cognitive-behavioral therapy. It is generally recognized as the best therapy for social anxiety.

In cognitive-behavioral therapy, a therapist helps you identify maladaptive thinking patterns and replace them with new ways of thinking. He or she also teaches you relaxation techniques and new behaviors that make you feel more comfortable in social situations.

Cognitive-behavioral therapy uses many of the same techniques that we explored in the previous chapter.

Although you might make great strides on your own, sometimes it is easier and faster to have someone guide you. Often it is difficult for people to explore hidden beliefs about themselves. A professional therapist is experienced in working with people who are trying to change. Often a therapist will see connections in your situation that you cannot.

Carlos was terrified of speaking in class. Whenever the teacher called on him, his heart raced, he blushed, and his stomach felt upset.

His therapist first had him focus on his thoughts during class. As an experiment, she had him purposely answer a question incorrectly during biology class. To his surprise, the teacher didn't make a big deal out of it, and the other students didn't laugh. As a result, Carlos realized that his imagined consequences for making errors were greatly exaggerated. He also realized that he held himself to a higher standard than other people, including the teacher, did.

Next, his therapist showed him various relaxation techniques to lessen the physical symptoms of anxiety. Soon, he felt more comfortable and even volunteered to lead a discussion group.

Group Therapy

Group therapy has been very successful for treating social anxiety, and there are many benefits to it. Members are a source of support for each other and the group allows you to address your fears in a safe environment. Listening to others' experiences helps you realize the ways in which social anxiety affects you. Group therapy also helps you become more comfortable speaking in front of people and sharing your thoughts. Moreover, it is typically less expensive than one-on-one therapy because group members share the cost.

There are also disadvantages to group therapy. You'll spend less time talking about your own problems than in one-on-one therapy. You might also worry about confidentiality. It is often difficult to trust that strangers aren't going to talk about your problems outside of the group. If you have this fear, it can be difficult to open up, thus lessening the effectiveness of group therapy.

Social Skills Training

Social skills training is based on the belief that socially anxious people lack certain social skills, such as how to make small talk or introduce themselves to strangers. Therapists think that anxiety would lessen for people if they knew the correct way to behave. In social skills training, you practice techniques such as rehearsal (practicing a certain skill until it becomes comfortable), modeling (imitating others in social situations until the behavior feels natural), and role playing. You also receive homework assignments, such as "This week, talk about the weather with three strangers."

A problem with this type of therapy is that even though many people know how they should act, they can't do it because of fear, negative thoughts, and avoidance. Although practicing social skills may take away some of the uncertainty, it doesn't address the deeper issues.

Hypnotherapy

You may have seen scenes on television in which hypnotists make people act like chickens or take off their clothes. In reality, hypnotherapy is nothing like that. You actually might experience a hypnotic state many times every week, or possibly every day. It is essentially no different than being engrossed in a book or movie, or being in the meditative state you may reach while exercising. During hypnosis you are highly focused and are not distracted by random thoughts. At the same time, you are aware of outside events, such as the telephone ringing or a door slamming.

When you see a hypnotherapist, he or she is simply a guide helping you reach a deeply relaxed state. The therapist may begin by having you picture a pleasant and safe environment. Or, he or she might ask you to focus on an object in your line of vision until your eyes become heavy.

Once you are in the hypnotized state, it is easier to focus on your anxiety. You can talk about past experiences, can work on your self-esteem, and can prepare for upcoming social events. You won't have distracting thoughts or be monitoring everything you say. You may remember events you had forgotten, or may come up with new ways to help yourself cope with the symptoms of anxiety.

Adriana was really nervous when her therapist suggested they use hypnosis to work on her fear of meeting new people, but she decided to try it. First, the therapist asked her to visualize a quiet place where she felt completely relaxed and comfortable. When Adriana's body felt heavy and warm, the therapist asked her to describe how she feels when she speaks with strangers. Adriana discussed how she feels embarrassed and worried, how her face gets red and hot, and how her mind is distracted by negative thoughts.

Next, the therapist asked Adriana to visualize being introduced to a stranger. She imagined herself feeling calm and relaxed and looking the person in the eyes. She rehearsed what she would say about herself and said it over and over, sounding more confident each time. The therapist then asked her to think of three things that could help her in those situations. Adriana decided to try relaxing, making sure she is breathing properly, and focusing on the other person instead of on her negative thoughts.

Later that week, she dined with a friend and his cousin, whom she had never met before. She was able to take deep breaths and remain relaxed. Once initial introductions went well, Adriana felt more confident and was able to maintain conversations for the entire evening.

Exposure Therapy

Exposure therapy, also known as desensitization, works best with very specific anxieties and phobias. For example, Jessica is deathly afraid of spiders. With the guidance of her therapist, she started exposure therapy by simply thinking about spiders. After she felt comfortable with that, she looked at pictures of various spiders and read about them. Next, she sat in a room with a spider. Gradually, the spider got closer and closer to her. With time, Jessica was able to let the spider crawl over her hand without being afraid. Gradually, she overcame her fear of spiders.

This type of therapy is most useful with specific social anxieties. Someone afraid of shopping could slowly work from walking into a store, to browsing, to trying clothes on, to making small talk with clerks, to buying something he or she likes. Someone afraid of writing in public could begin with small tasks such as signing a credit card receipt.

In exposure therapy, your therapist will have you spend as much time doing each step as it takes to feel comfortable with the action. At the same time, you will practice relaxation techniques. To be successful, you need to be able to be exposed to the event repeatedly without feeling anxiety.

Exposure therapy is less useful for generalized social anxiety. It is difficult to set up predictable scenarios for so many different situations. However, if you have generalized social anxiety and there is a particular area on which you want to focus, exposure therapy may be useful.

When trying exposure therapy, make sure not to use avoidance techniques to get through the task, such as "acting" in an appropriate way but feeling false, or going to a social event but not speaking with anyone new. Although it is better than nothing, simply getting through the activity will not give you the full benefit of desensitization.

Drug Therapy

Pharmaceutical companies have been developing new medications to eliminate the symptoms of social anxiety. The types of drugs available have increased and the newer medications have fewer side effects and are generally more effective than are the previous generation of drugs.

If your doctor or psychiatrist has suggested taking medication for your anxiety, you probably have many questions about side effects, how the drug works, and how long you have to take it. You should always discuss any questions or concerns about the drugs with your doctor.

Selective Serotonin Reuptake Inhibitors (SSRIs)

SSRIs were introduced in the late 1980s as antidepressants. They are the most prescribed class of drugs and have proven to be very effective at treating social anxiety. They work by blocking the uptake of the neurotransmitter serotonin into nerve cells. Serotonin is responsible for feelings of calmness and satisfaction. The most common SSRIs are Prozac and Paxil.

The benefits of SSRIs appear gradually, typically within four to eight weeks. They are free of most side effects because they affect only the neurotransmitter. They do not cause physical dependence and discontinuance does not cause withdrawal symptoms.

A concern with SSRIs is that they can cause dangerous reactions when combined with other prescription and over-the-counter medications. Make sure to check with your doctor or pharmacist before purchasing any other medication (including herbal supplements such as St. John's Wort) if you are taking an SSRI.

Beta-Blockers

Beta-blockers were the first type of medication used to treat anxiety. They work by blocking the beta-receptors for adrenaline, the hormone that creates excitement and stimulation. When adrenaline is blocked, it can't trigger symptoms such as a racing heart and shaking hands.

Beta-blockers are most successful when taken by someone with a specific social anxiety about an hour before the event or situation. People who take them report that the physical symptoms of anxiety are less intense and distracting.

These drugs are not as effective for people with generalized social anxiety when taken on a daily basis. This may be because they are more effective at blocking the physical symptoms than the mental symptoms.

The only restriction associated with beta-blockers is that they should not be given to people with asthma, diabetes, or certain forms of heart disease. Most people experience minimal side effects from beta-blockers. They are not addictive; however, they can become a crutch. For example, if you fear giving speeches, you may feel that you need to take a pill every time you speak.

Benzodiazepines

Instead of blocking beta-receptors like beta-blockers, benzodiazepines act directly on the anxiety signal at its origin, in the brain. This type of medication works effectively on both generalized and specific social anxiety. Valium and Xanax are the best-known examples.

People are usually directed to take benzodiazepines on a regular basis, two to four times per day. When they are taken regularly, the body adjusts to the drug and eventually the side effects diminish while the anti-anxiety effects remain. If benzodiazepines are taken on an as-needed basis, they tend to cause drowsiness and fatigue and can slow mental responses.

Because of the adjustment the body makes, a physical dependency on the drug develops. When the drug is discontinued, it must be done gradually. These drugs also have the potential to be abused. Because they can cause drowsiness, they can be used to escape the real world.

Monoamine Oxidase Inhibitors (MAOIs)

MAOIs, such as Nardil and Parnate, work by inhibiting the activity of the enzyme monoamine oxidase (MAO), which is an important regulator of several neurotransmitters in the brain. They are most useful for people with generalized social anxiety. In a controlled clinical study, researchers found that MAOIs increased confidence, created a higher resistance to criticism, and reduced overall anxiety.

However, because the side effects of MAOIs can be alarming, extreme caution must be taken when they are prescribed. Among other responses, they can react with chemicals in certain foods and cause the blood pressure to rise sharply. Other common side effects are drowsiness, dry mouth, and weight gain.

Stages of Therapy

No matter which type of therapy you use, treatment should have a definite course with a beginning, middle, and end. There is no set time limit on each stage. A person may have problems in a certain area and as a result, may need to spend more time in that stage of the process.

Because people with social anxiety have difficulty opening up, the first stage of therapy is devoted to establishing trust between you and your therapist. As trust and communication increase, you are ready to begin the next stage.

The middle phase of therapy is the most difficult. In psychoanalytical therapy, this phase begins when you realize the cause of tension in your life and the factors that have caused social anxiety. Feelings that have been deeply buried are openly discussed. In cognitive-behavioral therapy, the middle phase is when faulty thought patterns are changed and new behaviors are learned. As these new skills replace the disordered behaviors, you are ready to enter the last stage.

The final stage is when you move the coping skills you have learned in therapy into your real life, without the help of your therapist. It is common for some symptoms of anxiety to return as the uncertainty of dealing with social situations without therapy is realized. If you are truly ready to end therapy, you will have the confidence and trust in yourself to move forward in a healthy way.

Choosing a Therapist

There are many ways to go about choosing a therapist. One method is to call some of the organizations listed in the Where to Go for Help section of this book. Each will gladly send you a list of therapists in your area. Another method is to ask your school nurse or physician for a referral. They probably have dealt with this issue before and are familiar

The *Journal of Consulting and Clinical Psychology* lists four factors that need to be present for successful therapy.

1. There should be a clear understanding of the goals and aims of therapy, the role of the therapist, your responsibility, and the expected time frame of treatment.

2. The therapy should give you skills that you can use immediately to control your life in a healthy way.

3. The therapist should emphasize that you learn to use these skills independently of him or her.

4. The therapist should encourage you to see that progress is due to you and your actions, not to the therapist.

with people in the field. The yellow pages or local psychological referral services also provide names of therapists. However, because anyone can get a listing, you need to do a thorough background check.

The most important thing about finding a therapist is that you feel comfortable with that person. It doesn't matter how many degrees the therapist has or how many patients he or she has treated if you do not feel comfortable communicating with him or her.

People have a tendency to trust authority figures. If things aren't improving, they blame themselves instead of the expert. Remember, therapists are people with distinct personalities. Just as there are some people you find difficult to get along with, there will be therapists whom you don't like. If you find it hard to trust the therapist, you won't be able to open up and honestly discuss important issues. However, it is important not to use this as an excuse. The therapist will make you talk about some deep and possibly painful feelings. Although this may make you uncomfortable, it is not a reason to stop seeing that person.

A Final Word

Now that you have become familiar with social anxiety, you know that it is a common problem, especially for teenagers. You've learned that it affects you physically, mentally, and behaviorally, and that it can have a tremendous impact on all aspects of your life.

Most important, you've learned ways to cope with social anxiety. Now, make the techniques presented in this book part of your daily life. With practice you will be able to

Questions to Ask When Selecting a Therapist:

↪ How long have you been treating social anxiety?

↪ How many patients have you seen with my type of problem?

↪ How long does a therapy session usually last?

↪ What happens during the course of treatment?

↪ What can I expect from a typical session?

↪ What are your goals for therapy?

↪ What are your feelings about medication?

↪ What kind of follow-up care is available after therapy ends?

calm anxious feelings and develop self-confidence in social situations. Remember that change does not happen overnight. There will be tough times mixed in with the good. It may be necessary to see a professional therapist or to take medication.

There is no reason social anxiety needs to remain a part of your life. If you are committed to lessening your anxiety, you will see great results. With time and hard work, you can become the person you want to be and live a healthy, happy, and productive life.

Glossary

action plan A set of specific steps that will help you attain your goals.

anxiety A feeling of apprehension and fear that causes physical symptoms, maladaptive thoughts, and inappropriate behavior.

autogenic training A technique that helps you relax by making your body feel heavy and warm.

automatic thoughts Thoughts that you have so often that they seem instinctive and beyond your control.

avoidance Staying away from situations that make you nervous.

behavioral rehearsal Practicing your actions so you will feel comfortable in various situations.

catastrophizing Having unrealistic, negative beliefs about what will occur in a situation.

cognitive-behavioral therapy A type of therapy that focuses on changing to healthier ways of thinking and acting.

coping statements Short, easy-to-remember statements that help you cope with anxiety.

core beliefs Unconscious or conscious beliefs that influence how you feel about yourself and how you behave.

drug therapy Using medication to alleviate the symptoms of a condition.

freezing Being unable to act or speak.

generalized social anxiety Feeling anxious in a wide variety of social situations.

group therapy A type of therapy in which a group of people with similar problems discusses issues.

hypnotherapy The process of entering a relaxed state in which you can focus on certain issues.

long-term goal A goal that is difficult to achieve and that requires you to work on it for a long period of time.

maladaptive thinking patterns Ways of looking at a situation that have a negative effect on your mindset.

modeling Imitating the successful ways in which others act.

neurotransmitters Chemicals that carry messages from your brain to your body through a network of interconnecting cells.

paced breathing A technique that helps you take deep breaths from the diaphragm.

perfectionism Wanting to do everything with no mistakes or problems.

private self-consciousness Worrying about how you view yourself.

progressive muscle relaxation (PMR)   A technique that helps you relax by tensing various muscle groups, then releasing the tension.

psychoanalytic therapy   A type of therapy that focuses on talking about and understanding the underlying reasons that contribute to certain behavior.

public self-consciousness   Worrying about how others view you.

short-term goal   A goal that can be achieved in a short amount of time.

shyness   Feeling reserved and timid around other people.

social anxiety   A condition of feeling extremely self-conscious and afraid in social situations.

social skills training   Learning the correct way to behave in social situations.

specific social anxiety   Feeling anxious about a specific social event or task.

visualization   A technique that helps you replace maladaptive thoughts with relaxing scenes.

worst-case scenario technique   A technique in which you imagine the most terrible things that can happen in a situation in order to help you correct your inaccurate expectations.

Where to Go for Help

Hotlines

Boys Town USA
(800) 448-3000
A twenty-four hour crisis line for boys and girls.

National Mental Health Association Information Center (NMHA)
(800) 969-6642
An organization that provides referrals to local mental
  health offices.

(800) THERAPIST Network
(800) 843-7274
Provides referrals to local therapists

For More Information

American Academy of Child and Adolescent Psychiatry
3615 Wisconsin Avenue, NW
Washington, DC 20016-3007
(202) 966-7300
Web site: http://www.aacap.org

American Psychiatric Association
Public Affairs Office, Suite 501
1400 K Street, NW
Washington, DC 20005
(888) 357-7924
Web site: http://www.psych.org

American Psychological Association
750 First Street, NE
Washington, DC 20002-4242
(800) 964-2000
Web site: http://www.apa.org

National Institute of Mental Health
Information and Inquiries
6001 Executive Boulevard, Room 8184, MSC 9663
Behesda, MD 20892-9663
Web site: http://www.nimh.nih.gov/anxiety

Web Sites

The Anxiety Clinic of Arizona
http://www.anxietynetwork.com

Anxiety Disorder Association of America
http://www.adaa.org

The Social Anxiety Network
http://www.social-anxiety-network.com

Freedom From Fear
http://www.freedomfromfear.org

The Social Phobia/Social Anxiety Association
http://www.socialphobia.org

The Social Anxiety Support Group
http://www.socialanxietysupport.com

For Further Reading

Berent, Jonathan, and Amy Lemley. *Beyond Shyness: How to Conquer Social Anxieties.* New York: Simon & Schuster, 1993.

Markway, Barbara G, Cheryl N. Carmin, C. Alec Pollard, and Teresa Flynn. *Dying of Embarrassment: Help for Social Anxiety and Phobia.* Oakland, CA: New Harbinger Publications, Inc., 1992.

Marshall, John R. *Social Phobia: From Shyness to Stage Fright.* New York: Basic Books, 1994.

Rapee, Ronald M. *Overcoming Shyness and Social Phobia.* Northvale, NJ: Jason Aronson, 1998.

Schneier, Franklin and Lawrence Welkowitz. *The Hidden Face of Shyness.* New York: Avon Books, 1996.

Index

About the Author

Heather Moehn is a freelance writer and an editor in Boston, Massachusetts. Her nonfiction young adult books cover such diverse topics as world holidays, leukemia, and eating disorders. She has a B.A. in English from Carleton College.